At the Crossroads:
Ethical and Religous Themes
in the Writings of
Walker Percy

At the Crossroads:
Ethical and Religous Themes
in the Writings of
Walker Percy

by

John F. Desmond

The Whitston Publishing Company
Troy, New York
1997

Copyright 1997
John F. Desmond

Library of Congress Catalog Card Number 96-60695

ISBN 0-87875-480-6

Printed in the United States of America

JUL 1 4 1998

In memory of my parents,
Bridget and Richard Desmond,
and for all future readers of Walker Percy

Contents

Acknowledgements

I want to thank several friends and colleagues who have been especially supportive of my work: Gary Ciuba, Richard Giannone, Lewis A. Lawson, Patrick Samway, S.J., Joseph Schwartz, and Lewis P. Simpson.

I also want to thank Dean David Deal of Whitman College for his continuing encouragement of my scholarly endeavors.

I want to thank the following journals for publishing my essays and for allowing me to reprint them here:

"Love, Sex, and Knowledge in *Lancelot*," *Mississippi Quarterly* (Spring, 1986)

"Walker Percy and T. S. Eliot—the Lancelot Andrewes Connection," *The Southern Review* (Summer, 1986)

"Disjunctions of Time: Myth and History in *The Thanatos Syndrome*," *New Orleans Review* (December, 1989)

"Flannery O'Connor, Walker Percy, and the Holocaust," *The Southern Quarterly* (Winter, 1990)

"Signs of the Times: Lancelot and the Misfit," *The Flannery O'Connor Bulletin*, 18 (1989-90)

"Walker Percy and the Little Way," *Renascence* (Fall, 1991)

"From Suicide to Ex-Suicide: Notes on the Southern Writer as Hero in the Age of Despair," *Southern Literary Journal* (December, 1992)

"Revisioning *The Fall*: Walker Percy and *Lancelot*," *The Mississippi Quarterly* (Fall, 1994)

"Walker Percy's Triad: Science, Religion, and Literature," *Renascence* (Fall, 1995)

Introduction

A striking fact about Walker Percy as a man and as a writer was the enormous range of his intellectual interests and comprehension. While neither a professional theologian nor a philosopher, Percy had clearly absorbed the main lines of development in theology and philosophy in the West since the Middle Ages. He read deeply in St. Augustine and St. Thomas Aquinas, Pascal and Descartes, Kierkegaard, Sartre, Guardini, Barth, Heidegger and many other thinkers. His knowledge of science as both medical doctor and lay scientist was considerable. He took a special interest in the vexing question of the role of science and technology in modern culture, especially the threat it poses to the autonomy of the single human being. He was a serious and life-long student of linguistics, anthropology and history. He also knew well the major writings in American and European literature, particularly the tradition of the philosophical novel as shaped by Dostoevsky, Mann, Sartre and Camus.

Yet for Percy all this was not just a matter of intellectual curiosity or of achieving some kind of "Renaissance Man" status. Rather, he attempted to bring all this knowledge to bear on what he saw as the singular plight of his fellow creatures in the modern world. He wanted to diagnose our condition, and implicitly, to suggest a possible cure for the condition of alienation or "lostness" he saw—and personally felt—so vividly manifested in our century. Hence his novels and essays serve as crossroads or points of intersection where the main lines of intellectual and moral concern converge and focus on a central question: How can human beings live authentically in the twentieth century?

The essays I offer here are attempts to shed some light on these crossroads or points of intersection in Percy's writing—and to read his fiction and essays in light of the issues Percy confronted at these crossroads. And which we continue to confront. I try to examine his engagement with these issues and with the influential religious, philosophical, and literary figures who "lived" with Percy in a community of mutual concern and searching. These figures range from Jesus, St. Augustine, and St. Theresa of Liseux, to philosophers Søren Kierkegaard, St. Thomas Aquinas and Charles Sanders Peirce, to philosophical novelists Jean Paul Sartre and Albert Camus, and to fellow American writers William Faulkner, Flannery O'Connor, and Don Delillo. With them—and sometimes in opposition to them—Percy examines the pivotal religious and ethical issues of our age: suicide, euthanasia, vocation, scientism, the role of the artist, human sexuality, language, technology, community—and the most embracing issue of all: the "loss" of our sense of being as free creatures, and how we might recover being.

My hope is that these essays may help to bring the reader into that community of interest and concern Percy so brilliantly created in his writings, to make them fellow journeyers with Percy and his "friends" as he both reveals our predicament and paradoxically enriches our lives in the process.

Walker Percy and the Little Way

Midway in his life's journey in *The Moviegoer*, Binx Bolling is asked by his Uncle Jules to make a business trip to Chicago. Although he agrees to go, Binx anticipates the trip with considerable foreboding. He says: "Oh sons of all bitches and great beast of Chicago lying in wait. There goes my life in Gentilly, my Little Way, my secret existence among the happy shades in Elysian Fields."[1] Later in the novel, before his departure for Chicago, Binx muses upon his possible future life during a trip to the Gulf coast with his secretary Sharon Kincaid.

> But life goes on and on we go, spinning along the coast in a violet light, past Howard Johnsons and the motels and the childrens' carnival. We pull into a bay and have a drink under the stars. It's not a bad thing to settle for the Little Way, not the big search for the big happiness but the sad little happiness of drinks and kisses, a good little car and a warm deep thigh." (110-111)

Binx's life of easeful pleasure-seeking is soon to be jolted by the obligatory business trip, but as his later comment suggests, the real threat to this Little Way existence is his own recognition of the despair that underlies it, and the need for "the search" to overcome despair which that recognition inspires. As Binx declares during the train ride,

> (the) search has spoiled the pleasure of my tidy and ingenious life in Gentilly. As late as a week ago, such a phrase as "hopefully awaiting the gradual convergence of the physical sciences and the social sciences" would have provoked no more than an ironic tingle or two at the back of my neck. Now it howls through the Pontichula Swamp, the very sound and soul of despair. (152-153)

The opposition Binx establishes between the comfortable life of the Little Way and the life of the "search" is apparently complete. To settle for what Binx calls "the sad little happiness of drinks and kisses, a good little car and a warm deep thigh" is to abandon "the big search for the big happiness." But Binx's discovery of despair within his Little Way existence tells us that things are never so simple or unequivocal in Percy's fictive world. Percy is one of the most elusive and cunning American writers, a fact both necessitated and conditioned by the deep religious sensibility that informs his work. Binx's awareness of despair shows us, in fact, that the real issue is not one of choosing *between* the quotidian world of the Little Way and the life of the search, but rather one of pursuing "the big search for the big happiness" *within* the sad little world of "drinks and kisses, a good little car and a warm deep thigh." The issue, then, is one of vocation, understood in the widest sense as religious in nature. How Percy confronts this issue is crucial for understanding both Binx's final commitments in *The Moviegoer*, and beyond that, for understanding Percy's vocation as novelist, characteristics of which are projected into Binx Bolling's struggle to reconcile the demands of the "big search for the big happiness" with the quotidian world of the Little Way.[2]

Percy's development of the ideas of the search and the Little Way through Binx's narration is oblique and ironic, yet serious. Binx never claims explicitly that the search is a search for God. Indeed he says his "unbelief (is) invincible" because "he could never make head or tail of God" (119). At the same time, Binx says that it is impossible to rule God out, and that the only sign of God now "is that all the signs in the world make no difference," which may be God's ironic revenge; yet Binx concludes: "But I am onto him" (119). Similarly, Binx both praises and denigrates the life of the Little Way. It is both a life of comfortable *bonhomie* and a healthy antidote to the alienation of longing for the transcendent; but it is also the locus of despair. What to make of this mystery?

Although Binx's descriptions of his life in Gentilly are tinged with bemused irony, it is difficult to contemplate Percy's use of the notion of the Little Way without recalling the most famous modern use of that idea in relation to the problem of religious vocation—that is, in the *Autobiography* of St. Theresa of Lisieux, the Carmelite nun known as St. Theresa of the Child Jesus who died of tuberculosis in 1897 and was canonized a saint in 1925. Enclosed in the small world of the religious cloister, Theresa developed her life of the Little Way as a spiritual discipline for living in the world, and the nature of that discipline is worth contemplating in relation to Binx Bolling and to Percy himself as novelist.

Theresa entered the Carmelite convent in 1888 at age fifteen; she became a novice the following year and professed her final vows in 1890. Her *Autobiography* shows that Theresa grew up imbued with a rather inflated, heroic dream of sanctity and martyrdom. For some time she wanted to become a missionary, a dream never fulfilled, partly because of the poor health which was eventually to end her life at age twenty-four. But during her years in the convent, Theresa's once-heroic ideal of spirituality underwent a radical transformation, one which brought her to understand her vocation in a new way. Instead of aspiring to heroic sanctity and martyrdom, Theresa began to understand that the path to God lay in complete self-surrender to the minute humiliations, sufferings, and joys of every moment, every day. She developed, as Barry Ulanov has shown, an intense devotion to "littleness," an obsession with finding the will of God in the seemingly most inconsequential details and trails of everyday existence. Her vocation now became to make herself "little," to strive for a humble self-abandonment to the divine will. Theresa's model for this *kenosis* was Jesus Himself, who as God undertook a total abasement in becoming human and uniting Himself with every detail of creaturely existence.

However, Theresa's discipline of the Little Way, as she came to call it, was not one of stoic resignation or masochistic self-denial. As Monica Furlong explains, Theresa "saw that all you were asked to do was to follow the will of God, whatever it might be, and give yourself unreservedly to *that* life and to no other . . ," because "she realized that instead of trying to be something she was not—a crusader or an Apostle—she was now free to be Theresa with all her little problems."[3] Following the will of God did not mean groveling before humiliations; rather, it meant viewing herself from a great distance and seeing the ordinary humiliations of life as a sign of human imperfection. Nor did it mean a passive acceptance of evil and sin; rather, it meant a daily *kenotic* struggle to see that condition from a perspective of divine mercy and charity. "Humility is truth," Theresa affirmed.[4]

The key to her spiritual discipline was love manifested in charity, a love that transformed a life of resignation and constraint into joy. Her goal was a mortification of the will, a total relinquishment of personal desire to the will of God. But to practice the Little Way required a constant daily struggle and suffering, a struggle in which nothing was guaranteed. It was, in effect, a search undertaken to discover the will of God and to unite herself to it. This was coupled with a constant celebration of the ordinary given world, especially the world of nature and its small daily revelations of beauty and mystery. "Ah, let us profit, profit by the shortest instant (Theresa says), act like misers, be jealous of the smallest things for the sake of the Beloved!" (*Ulanov*, 150). Finally, Theresa's Little Way did not require a suppression of consciousness; on the contrary, consciousness is central to the discipline since it demands a constant, knowing attention to what one is doing and why. Such persistent attention is to be focussed on those unconscious tendencies in the self that prohibit the practice of love. This struggle became the real interior ordeal of her Little Way. As Theresa proclaimed: "My vocation is love."

Theresa's life in the cloister at Carmel and her spiritual discipline may seem too remote or antiquated a vision for the post-modern, post-Christian world of the late 20th century, but to assume so, as Ulanov argues, is to miss the vitality and relevancy of her spirituality.

> To miss the way Theresa applies her way of littleness and weakness and humble disposition to the trivia of her life—the nagging little irritations, the constant minor vexations, the creepy-crawly afflictions—is to miss her genius for dealing with the human condition as it generally and inevitably must irritate and vex and afflict us all. To miss it is to fail to understand how one can lift oneself above the tiny despondencies that far more than any one great terror lead one to despair. (293)

Compared to St. Theresa's discipline, Binx Bolling's Little Way existence of pleasure-seeking in Gentilly may seem an ironic travesty of Theresan spirituality. Nevertheless, Binx's idea of the "horizontal search," his meticulous attention to the wonders of the world around him, to the details of movie-going and movie-watching, and especially his attention to others, suggest a more serious application of the idea of the Little Way at work in the novel, especially when Binx affirms the search both as an antidote to the "everydayness" that threatens to "cancel out" the reality of the quotidian world, and as the ironic starting point for pursuing the God whom he is "onto." Binx may claim that the ordinary world is canceled-out by everydayness, but his actual narration (the mask for Percy the author)—with its meticulous and joyous attention to the details of existence—totally reverses his argument (as Percy said in his essay "The Man on the Train," the *story* about alienation reverses that condition).[5] Viewed in this way, Binx's horizontal search *through* the quotidian world suggests a starting point for a strategy of existence that is at least incipiently Theresan in spirit.

Nevertheless, important distinctions must be kept in mind while claiming some affinity between *The Moviegoer* and the *Autobiography* of St. Theresa. Percy's novel is a highly enigmatic work of fiction; Theresa's autobiography is an attempt to disclose the contours of her spiritual life. More importantly, Theresa's Little Way is a religious discipline developed consciously as a means to approach God, a God whose presence she, as a believer, affirms unequivocally. Binx Bolling, on the other hand, says he cannot make "head or tail" of God, and he separates himself from both believers and unbelievers by claiming for himself the role of searcher. Given these distinctions, it would be mistaken to conclude that Percy's intention in *The Moviegoer* is to create in Binx a kind of covert believer *malgri lui*. Such a claim would effectively destroy the rich ambiguity of the novel, ambiguity that often is focussed particularly on the mysteries of spirituality and vocation.

Nevertheless, the Theresan discipline of the Little Way seems to resonate mysteriously within the novel in several ways. If we look for an explicit example of the Theresan discipline in the novel—of the believer striving to live the Little Way—it is to be found in the figure of Lonnie Smith, Binx's debilitated half-brother. Lonnie struggles to transform the enforced constraints of his life into joy precisely by a loving concentration on the small routines of everyday life in a manner that is quintessentially Theresan, whether in playing "Akim Tamiroff" with Binx, listening to his transistor radio, fasting to overcome an "habitual disposition" to envy his dead brother Duvall, sharing the sacred joy of watching "Ft. Dobbs" at the Moonlite Drive-in with Binx and Sharon, or receiving holy communion. Binx has a special love for Lonnie, a youth who like Theresa "has the gift of believing that he can offer his sufferings in reparation for men's indifference to the pierced heart of Jesus Christ. For another thing (Binx says), I would not mind so much trading places with him. His life is a serene business" (112).

In contrast to Lonnie, his mother Mrs. Smith has developed her own diminished "little way" existence. She is nominally a believer, but as Binx notices she uses God for "the canny management of the shocks of life." Having lost her favorite son Duvall, she has "settled for a general belittlement of everything, the good and the bad." Losing Duvall, Binx says, has "confirmed her in her election of the ordinary. No more heart's desire for her, thank you. After Duvall's death she has wanted everything colloquial and easy, even God" (116). Mrs. Smith's "little way," unlike Lonnie's, is a joyless stoic resignation to loss in which the idea of God and the commonplace is "used" to "manage" the despair that threatens her in every detail of existence. In effect, she has abandoned any search for the numinous within the commonplace world. Not for her any of Lonnie and Binx's rejoicing in the minutae of life, or that joyful self-abandonment to the wonder and mystery of the quotidian world that Lonnie and Binx enjoy and which St. Theresa saw as the path to love and freedom.

Binx's own spiritual disposition, it seems to me, lies somewhere between that of his mother and his half-brother Lonnie, but increasingly as the novel unfolds Binx moves closer to Lonnie's self-abandoning mode of spiritual discipline. Binx's self-indulgent Little Way existence in Gentilly can be seen as a more sophisticated and pleasurable version of the "management of the shocks" of life practiced by his mother, yet equally despairing. On the other hand, Binx's desire to pursue the search, to be "onto" God by uncovering clues and signs in the minutae of life, and by rejoicing in their mystery, echoes much of Lonnie's daily spiritual routine in substance if not by explicit religious definition. Hence their close friendship. And significantly, Binx is often recalled to the "search" after disturbing experiences of symbolic self-annihilation—first in the Korean War, then at the Smith's cottage when he learns about his father's fruitless search that eventually led to his death in World War II, and finally near the end of the novel when his comfortable life in Gentilly collapses completely.

Binx's movement toward the deeper reality of the Theresan Little Way practiced by Lonnie is intimated particularly by his final choice of vocation and his marriage to Kate Cutrer.

From a Theresan point of view it matters little whether, as Binx puts it, "this vocation is best pursued in a service station or—" by practicing medicine, since the inner reality of his vocation will be to "listen to people, see how they stick themselves into the world, hand them along a ways in their dark journey and be handed along, and for good and selfish reasons" (184). This last phrase—"for good and selfish reasons"—would seem to deny the ideal of self-abandonment that St. Theresa expresses as the goal of her spiritual discipline. But not necessarily, if Binx's pro- claimed "selfishness" is in fact a vocation of service to others.

Of course, what is missing from Binx's discussion of his vocation (as distinct from his profession) is St. Theresa's *explicit* linking of her Little Way of spirituality to the person of God in Jesus. Binx rarely mentions God or Jesus, though he says the possibility of God cannot be ruled out. Nevertheless, he does implicitly affirm the divine reality, the source of a vision of the transfiguration of the common, ordinary world, when he tells Lonnie's brothers and sisters that Lonnie will be renewed in body after the final resurrection from the dead. But Percy usu- ally states the possibility obliquely, as oblique as Binx's uncer- tainty about whether or not the Negro man emerging from the church on Ash Wednesday is a sign of God's presence.

> It is impossible to say why he is here. Is it part and parcel of the complex business of coming up in the world? Or is it because he believes that God himself is present here at the corner of Elysian Fields and Bons Enfants? Or is he here for both reasons: through some dim dazzling trick of grace, coming for the one and re- ceiving the other as God's own importunate bonus?
> It is impossible to say. (186)

It is, as Binx declares, "impossible to say." Not that it is impossible, but that it is impossible *to say*, which is precisely where the novelist must remain true to the mystery before him, and forego turning fiction into apologetics.

Although the Theresan ideal of the Little Way may be only obliquely hinted at in Binx's final commitment to marriage and a medical career, the *spiritual discipline* and attentiveness it demands toward the mystery of the quotidian world is directly relevant to the vocation of the writer with religious concerns, and so to Percy's vocation as a novelist. Binx's "horizontal search" into the wonder of the ordinary can be seen, of course, as a fictional mask for Percy's own search as novelist into the ordi- nary. In this regard Binx's final stance towards the issue of the numinous in the concrete world—his "impossible to say" whether God is present, yet his belief that the reality of God cannot be ruled out—may be taken as an image of Percy the writer's stance toward the quotidian world which it is his vocation to explore. Percy on several occasions has described the writer as an "ex-suicide," a "nought" who empties himself in an act of *kenosis* before the minutae of existence until, lost in self-surrender, he is mysteriously granted a way to transfigure the canceled-out details of a four o'clock Thursday afternoon into vivified reality.

Percy's description of the humbling self-abandonment demanded in the writer's vocation echoes St. Theresa's humble search for the divine in the smallest details of existence as she practiced the Little Way. Percy has suggested, in typically wry fashion, that the gift the writer receives in the moment of self-surrender to "nought"-ness may in fact be a divine grace, a grace he described as a miraculous revelation of the numinous within the quotidian world. In his 1977 self-interview in *Esquire*, Percy said:

> The best novels, and the best part of a novel, is a *creatio ex nihilo*. Unlike God, the novelist does not start with nothing and make something of it. He starts with himself as nothing and makes something of the nothing with things at hand. . . . A novelist these days has to be an ex-suicide. A good novel . . . is possible only after one has given up and let go. . . . Let us say a writer finds himself at 0, nought, zero, at 4 p.m. on Thursday afternoon. No energy, depressed, strung out, impotent, constipated, a poet sitting on the kitchen floor with the oven door open and the gas on, an incarnated nothingness, an outer human husk encasing an inner cipher. The jig is up. Then, if he is lucky—or is it grace, God having mercy on the poor bastard?—something opens. A miracle occurs. Somebody must have found the Grail. The fisher king is healed, the desert turns green—or better still: the old desert is still the old desert but the poet names it and makes it a new desert.[6]

Later, in a 1980 interview with Dannye Romine, Percy made a similar point about the mystery of writing: "What I'm telling you is, I don't know anything. It's a question of being so pitiful God take pity on you, looks down and says: 'He's done for. Let's let him have a couple of good sentences'" (202).

One can argue that any artist undergoes such self-emptying before the concrete world in order to create. True enough—but *how* the writer sees and vivifies the details of existence is the crucial question, and here Percy's difference seems to me to lie in his fidelity to, his joyous affirmation of, the quotidian as *the very means*—the Little Way—*through* which his vocation as religious novelist can be fulfilled, and more importantly as the only means through which the human search for a transfiguring spirit that gives the humblest reality its integrity and brings with it the loving serenity of a Lonnie Smith, can be fulfilled.   The problem is put best perhaps by Percy's figure of grace in The *Second Coming*, Alison Huger:

> All this time she had made a mistake. She had thought . . . that she must do something extraordinary, be somebody extraordinary. Whereas the trick lay in leading the most ordinary life imaginable, get an ordinary job, in itself a joy in its very ordinariness, and *then* be as extraordinary or ordinary as one pleased. That was the secret.[7]

Allie's insight is precisely that discovered by St. Theresa in her early years at Carmel. Like Fr. John in *Lancelot* and Fr. Rinaldo Smith in *The Thanatos Syndrome*, she returns to the ordinary after a spectacular "flame-out" attempt at transcendence.

As a novelist Percy does not make any explicit connection between humble attentiveness to the trivia of existence and the search for God-in-Jesus as St. Theresa does in her *Autobiography*. Nevertheless, implicit in his commitment to the quotidian is his Christian recognition that nothing is ever lost, and that even the most obscure and seemingly insignificant of actions or signs can be the "Little Way" that opens to a saving truth. St. Theresa saw God in a grain of sand; Percy attempts to do likewise insofar as he affirms the incredible wonder and mystery of the smallest things, as signs that open reality to the numinous.

As Percy often noted, it is not the novelist's job to directly edify, particularly in a time when the language of belief is largely bankrupt. Yet it is here—in the use of language as sign—that Percy conducts his search and suggests the mysterious interpenetration of the quotidian and the numinous, what Flannery O'Connor called the action of grace. In his vocation he became that "nought," that ex-suicide who empties himself to become the Namer who discovers the mystery of the thing-in-itself, and that reality beyond itself to which it points. Language and sign are his means to reconcile the "big search" and the "sad little life" of four o'clock Thursday afternoons, by naming the ordinary reality with such fidelity, such joy, and such loving attention to its worthiness so as to suggest the existence of an ultimate

Name-giver. The Little Way of attentiveness becomes a sign of vocation both for the novelist, and for any reader who searches, as St. Theresa did, for an encounter with the divine Other in the most ordinary details of everyday existence.

Notes

[1] Percy, Walker. *The Moviegoer.* New York: Avon Books, 1960, p. 82. All further references cited in the text.

[2] Letter to Shelby Foote, dated ca. 1966. From the Percy-Shelby Foote letters, Library of the University of North Carolina, Chapel Hill, NC ". . . I keep thinking that it is always possible to do the BIG ONE, bigger than Don Quixote, Moby Dick, et. al.—which is the shortest path to melancholy and perdition, since as St. Theresa of the Little Flower used to say, the only road is the Little Way, viz. the only way to do great things is to choose to treat little things well. The other path leads to grandiosity of spirit, flatulence of the creative process, and perdition in general."

[3] Furlong, Monica. *Theresa of Liseux.* New York: Pantheon Books, 1987, p. 96.

[4] Ulanov, Barry. *The Making of a Modern Saint.* Garden City, NY: Doubleday & Co., 1966, p. 196.

[5] Percy, Walker. "The Man on the Train," in *The Message in the Bottle.* New York: Farrar, Straus and Giroux, 1975, pp. 83-101.

[6] Percy, Walker. "Questions They Never Asked Me," in *Conversations with Walker Percy.* Jackson: University of Mississippi Press, 1985, pp. 164-165.

[7] Percy, Walker. *The Second Coming.* New York: Farrar, Straus and Giroux, 1980, p. 247.

Binx Bolling—
Walker Percy's Musing Scientist

I.

Early in *The Moviegoer*, Binx Bolling describes the time in college when he abandoned scientific research. He and a friend named Harry Stern were spending part of the summer analyzing the role of acid-base balance in the formation of renal calculi, in order to examine the formation and dissolution of kidney stones in pigs. But then, Binx says, "a peculiar thing" happened:

> I became extraordinarily affected by the summer afternoons in the laboratory. The August sunlight came streaming in the great dusty fanlights and lay in yellow bars across the room. The old building ticked and creaked in the heat. . . . I became bewitched by the presence of the building; for minutes at a stretch I sat on the floor and watched the motes rise and fall in the sunlight. I called Harry's attention to the presence but he shrugged and went on with his work. He was absolutely unaffected by the singularities of time and place. His abode was anywhere. It was all the same to him whether he catheterized a pig at four o'clock in the afternoon in New Orleans or at midnight in Transylvania. He was actually like one of those scientists in the movies who don't care about anything but the problem in their head—now here is a fellow with a 'flair for research' and will be heard from. Yet I do not envy him. I would not change places with him if he discovered the cause and cure of cancer. For he is no more aware of the mystery which surrounds him than a fish is aware of the water it swims in. He could do research for a thousand years and never have an inkling of it. By the middle of August I could not see what difference it made whether the pigs got kidney stones or not (they didn't, incidentally), compared to the mystery of sum-

mer afternoons. I asked Harry if he would excuse me. He was glad enough to, since I was not much use to him sitting on the floor. I moved down to the Quarter where I spent the rest of the vacation in quest of the spirit of summer and in the company of an attractive and confused girl from Bennington who fancied herself a poet.[1]

Binx's experience in the laboratory underscores his (and Percy's) concern with the depersonalizing effects of doing scientific research. Later in the novel, Binx describes this effect in more general and disturbing terms when he discusses the "research" he is conducting in his own life. Reading a book called *Arabia Deserta*, he says:

There was a time when this was the last book on earth I'd have chosen to read. Until recent years, I read only 'fundamental' books, that is, key books on key subjects, such as *War and Peace*, the novel of novels; *A Study of History*, the solution of the problem of time; Shroedinger's *What is Life?*, Einstein's *The Universe As I See It*, and such. During those years I stood outside the universe and sought to understand it. I lived in my room as an Anyone living Anywhere and read fundamental books and only for diversion took walks around the neighborhood and saw an occasional movie. Certainly it did not matter to me where I was when I read such a book as *The Expanding Universe*. The greatest success of this enterprise, which I call my vertical search, came one night when I sat in a hotel room in Birmingham and read a book called *The Chemistry of Life*. When I had finished it, it seemed to me that the main goals of my search were reached or were in principle reachable, whereupon I went out and saw a movie called 'It Happened One Night' which was itself very good. A memorable night. The only difficulty was that though the universe had been disposed of, I myself was left over. There I lay in my hotel room with my search over yet still obliged to draw one breath and then the next. But now I have undertaken a different kind of search, a horizontal search. As a consequence, what takes place in my room is less important. What is important is what I shall find when I leave my room and wander in the neighborhood. Before, I wandered as a diversion. Now I wander seriously and read as a diversion. (69-70)

Readers familiar with Percy's essays and interviews recognize in Binx's remark Percy's criticism (echoing Kierkegaard) of that type of research which purports to explain the world in objective terms, yet cannot explain what it means to live and die as an individual in such a world. In addition, Binx's situation echoes the predicament of the scientist which Percy examined in *Lost in the Cosmos*, especially the scientist's problem of "reentry" into the ordinary world after experiencing transcendence through scientific research. For all its glories and achievements, scientific· research, as Percy shows, can become a mode of escape from the concrete self.[2] The very methods of scientific research—extrapolating from particulars, formulating hypotheses—seems to impoverish the concrete, existential self. Thus at this early point in the novel Binx sharply contrasts two modes of exploring reality: the way of traditional scientific inquiry—the "vertical search"; and a phenomenological approach, which is concrete and particular and includes the inquirer in the field of study—the "horizontal search." Whether the two approaches are in any sense reconcilable, and if so, how, is it seems to me a major question raised in *The Moviegoer*.

Despite Binx's ironic tone, Percy's intention in the novel is not to discredit traditional science. Percy frequently expressed admiration for genuine scientific research, in spite of his strong criticism of the idolatry of modern scientism. He also practiced science throughout his career—not as a physician—but as a scientific and imaginative inquirer into human behavior, especially language behavior. Moreover, as his essay "The Fateful Rift: The San Andreas Fault and the Modern Mind" makes clear, Percy believed firmly that a genuine science of man could be developed, one in which true knowledge could be derived from the empirical study of human behavior.[3] And finally, for all of Binx's proclaimed preference for "horizontal" over "vertical" searching, he does take up the study of medicine at the end of the novel, a career much dependent upon scientific research and method. His career as physician becomes the core of his announced vocation to "listen to people, see how they stick themselves into the world, hand them along a ways in their dark journey and be handed along, and for good and selfish reasons" (233). What, then, are we to make of Binx's initial opposition of vertical and horizontal searches or modes of inquiry, and their seeming convergence in Binx's final choice of vocation? In *The Moviegoer*, I would argue, Percy is attempting to examine the nature of the scientific enterprise within the broader context of human religious aspiration.

To help illuminate Percy's arguments about science in the novel and to shed light on Binx's development, I want to suggest some strong parallels between Percy's ideas and certain ideas developed by the American philosopher Charles Sanders Peirce. Percy's acknowledged debts to Peirce as a semioticist are well known. Peirce's triadic theory of knowledge form the basis of many of Percy's concepts of language developed in *The Message in the Bottle*, in *Lost in the Cosmos* and in his novels. Percy's study of Peirce dates at least from the mid-1950's, several years before the publication of *The Moviegoer*. His essay "Semiotic and a Theory of Knowledge," first published in 1957, reveals his familiarity with Peirce's thought.[4] What has not been fully explored as yet is the correspondence of their thought in other more general areas of philosophy which derive from semiotics.

Both Peirce and Percy believed in the fundamental compatibility between genuine science and its purposes, and religion. More specifically, both believed in the compatibility of Christianity with the goals and methods of genuine science. Both believed in a scientifically-based anthropology of man rooted in semiotic and the tradition of philosophical realism. Both believed that the human encounter with God was principally through natural signs, though inherently surrounded by mystery (or what Peirce called "vagueness"). Where Percy differs from Peirce in this regard is in his implicit linking of this philosophical vision to the incarnational and sacramental vision of Judeo-Christianity, especially in some of his later essays.[5] Finally, Peirce's fundamental concepts of abduction and musement as modes of inquiry, as I hope to show, are especially apposite Binx's spiritual and scientific searchings in *The Moviegoer*, as well as being important clues to Percy's own novelistic strategy.

II.

For Peirce, genuine scientific inquiry is governed by the principle of abduction, the cognitive process by which hypotheses or new ideas are created. Abduction is an innate "guessing instinct" which forms the basis of all scientific inquiry. "Abduction always involves observation, the imaginative manipulation of observed facts, and the formation of explanatory hypotheses."[6]

Percy stressed the significance of Peirce's concept of abduction in his essay "A Theory of Language." Here, Percy emphasized

> "how Peirce distinguished abduction from induction and deduction, the other two logical components of the scientific method. He believed that neither deduction nor induction could arrive at explanatory theory but only abduction. No new truth can come from deduction or induction. Deduction explores theological consequences of statements. Induction seeks to establish facts. Abduction starts from facts and seeks an explanatory theory."[7]

Abduction is a specific form of what Peirce called musement, which he defined as a process of reasoning which "involves no purpose save that of casting aside all serious purposes . . ." (CP 6.458). It is a kind of intellectual "Pure Play" governed by no rules except the "law of liberty" (CP 6.458). Musement, for Peirce, is not only central to scientific inquiry. It is also at the heart of the religious quest. As Peirce states, the muser's goal is not to become "convinced of the truth of religion" per se, but rather to contemplate "some wonder in one of the Universes, or some connection between two of the three" so that "religious meditation be allowed to grow spontaneously out of Pure Play without any breach of continuity" (CP 6.458).[8]

While it is impossible to discuss in detail here Peirce's scientific theism, it is important to emphasize the integral relation between his philosophy of science, his semiotic, and his theology. For Peirce, nature and its laws are embodiments of God's ideas. Peirce argued that "the universe is a vast representamen, a great symbol of God's purpose, working out its conclusions in living realities" (CP 5.119). For Peirce, the purpose of science in the broadest sense is to understand the representamen of God. Although he maintained that the muser does not set out initially to discover God, Peirce believed that musement does lead eventually to a realization of the naturalness of the reality of God. ". . . the idea of God's reality will be sure sooner or later to be found an attractive fancy, which the muser will develop in various ways. The more he ponders it, the more it will find repose in every part of his mind, for its beauty, for its supplying an idea of life, and for its thoroughly satisfying explanation of his whole threefold environment" (CP 6. 456).

The practice of science is a specific form of musement, as I noted. But the starting point for the muser and the scientist are the same—freely practiced abduction. The difference between the muser and the scientist, for Peirce, is whether the free play of meditation by the muser is converted into the disciplined study by the scientist. Still, for Peirce it is the muser who is in many ways the ideal scientist, the true searcher, one who defers all specific purposes and preconceptions to begin "inquiring in scientific singleness of heart" (CP 6.458). The muser is free because he is concerned with the *whole* of reality, what Peirce called "the collective total of all that is in any way present to the mind" (CP 1.284).

Peirce also affirmed the intrinsic relation between musement and ethical commitment, an important point for understanding the inner dynamic of Binx Bolling's search (see CP 8.262). Peirce maintained that the beauty of an idea, especially the idea of God, acted as a force influencing "the whole conduct of life." Musement leads the muser to *constructive pragmatic action* in the world. Binx Bolling's musements, I would argue, have precisely such an effect in his final choice of career and vocation.

However, several important qualifications regarding Peirce's concepts need to be made. First of all, while Peirce affirmed that musement leads to a realization of the naturalness of the idea of God, this was not to be construed as an ontological "proof" of God's existence. Peirce asserted that the idea of God attained through musement was necessarily "vague," though no less real for that. Although "we cannot think any thought of God's, we can catch a fragment of His thought as it were." Vagueness is a positive quality in Peirce's thought. As Robert Corrington argues,

> "If our basic beliefs are unconscious (as Peirce held) and are part of the general nature of instincts, and if instincts are themselves somewhat vague in terms of their specific issue in a given case, then it follows that our primitive and indubitable beliefs are vague. In fact, if these facts were anything *but* vague, they would make it difficult for the self to function in a variety of situations, each with its own complex variables. Vagueness thus has a deep evolutionary value." (55)

Secondly, Peirce recognized that the faculty of musement is also fallible. Circumstances, disposition, and flaws in the thinking process (eg. faulty perceptions, biases, errors in logic, misinterpretations of signs, etc.) can subvert the genuine free exercise of the faculty of musement. And thirdly, Peirce acknowledged that the faculty of musement could atrophy, making it nearly impossible for a person to exercise it. Significantly, Peirce's recognition of this condition of atrophy echoes a similar view expressed by Percy in his essay "Notes for a Novel about the End of the World," when he questioned whether the modern mind has become so saturated with the spirit of scientism's "tempestuous restructuring of consciousness" that it "does not presently allow (man) to take account of the Good News" (113). Likewise, in "The Culture Critics," Percy specified this condition even more in relation to Christianity when he described Western man's predicament as "this very incapacity to attach significance to the sacramental and historical-incarnational nature of Christianity" (269-270). Binx Bolling describes that he lives in "the very century of merde, the great shithouse of scientific humanism where needs are satisfied, everyone becomes an anyone, a warm and creative person, and prospers like a dung beetle, and one hundred percent of people are humanist and ninety-eight percent believe in God, and men are dead, dead, dead . . ." (MG, 228).

III.

Binx Bolling's idea of the search and his distinction between vertical and horizontal searches can be correlated, I believe, with Peirce's scientific theism in general and his concept of musement in particular. Binx's experience while doing research with Harry Stern, when he became fascinated with the wonders of the day and lost interest in the experiment, is clearly an experience of musement. Although superficially it appears that Binx has been beguiled into frivolous distraction, in fact he is acting as a serious muser who suddenly becomes aware of "the collective total of all that is in any way present to the mind." However, his rejection of the kind of research Harry Stern is engaged in is not a rejection of science understood in the broadest sense. Rather, Binx is caught by the nagging paradox of scientific investigation Percy elucidated in *Lost in the Cosmos*: that on the one hand it is exciting activity in which the researcher transcends the ordinary routines of life, but on the other it is so all-consuming that it threatens to negate the reality of the self doing the research (160-167). Since for Peirce all reality is continuous, and the role of the scientist is to interpret the representamen of God, research is a triadic event involving interpreter, phenom-

ena to be interpreted, and the symbol-language of interpretation.
A danger of the "vertical" search, a result of the Cartesian split
between mind and reality, it that it ignores the *total* triadic reality—the true semiotic—of the situation, particularly the non-
material but nevertheless real relationship between the re-
searcher, the phenomena being studied, and the larger *meaning*
of the laws of nature being examined. In short, this is a practice
of science disconnected from any consideration of nature as a
representamen of the mind of God. It denies the full semiotic of
the situation.   Likewise, it objectifies the researcher, preten-
tiously inflating his role into God-like status, while robbing him
of full humanity—the classic situation of gnosis.

Binx senses the reductiveness of the self implicit in the
vertical approach. As he says, it matters not to Harry Stern
whether he catheterizes pigs in New Orleans or Transylvania, at
four in the afternoon or at midnight. Binx's reaction, however,
is extreme. At this early stage in his journey he rejects a type of
research which has validity within a certain scientific context, in
favor of what he calls his horizontal search. As he says, he will
"not for five minutes be distracted from the wonder" (MG, 42).
Here, Binx sharply opposes a Peircean concept of musement, particularly musement open to the idea of God, to the empirical
method of modern science. Binx's journey in the novel will be
toward reconciling these dichotomous approaches to reality, or
in other words, to learn to practice empirical science—
medicine—within the larger vocation of being a "scientist" of all
reality, a muser in relation to God, and mankind. Binx must
discover how to link his true vocation, i.e. listening to others
and helping them along in the journey, with his career as a
physician.

Binx's horizontal search as a muser is fraught with far
more serious perils than simply being misunderstood by those
around him. For one, he is inclined to forget the search. First
awakened to the possibility of the search during the Korean War
while lying under a chindolea bush with the "queasy-quince
taste of 1951 and the Orient" in his mouth, Binx vows that if he
survives he will pursue the search. But "Naturally, as soon as I
recovered and got back home, (he admits) I forgot all about it"
(11). Binx gave up the free and sovereign stance of the muser for
the unreflective, comfortable life of the conformist living in
Gentilly among the other "dead" citizens unattuned to the

search. Yet as the novel opens Binx again awakens to the search and begins to muse.

Binx's narrative—his musings—is of a piece with Percy's fictional technique in *The Moviegoer*. The narrative strategy itself can be seen in some sense as an extensive musement. Binx is fascinated by the wonder of reality. Although Percy often described his narrative strategy in phenomenological and existential terms—placing a character "in a predicament"—it also seems appropriate to describe it as a form of musement. The novel's discursive movement certainly opens Binx's mind to a consideration of "the collective total of all that is in any way present to the mind" (CP 1.284). In his wandering and sifting through the phenomena of his experiences, encoded in signs, Binx keeps returning to the possibility of God, and he connects the signs he encounters in the world (like his thoughts on the Jews) with that possibility. He also keeps an open mind about the God hypothesis without being able to confirm it empirically. So also Percy holds out the possibility of God "vaguely" (to use Peirce's concept) in the novel, encoded in oblique actions and signs. Narratively, then, the novel can be seen as an "experiment" in Peircean musement, a "scientific" study in the broadest sense of the signs of God and His universe.

Just as the vertical search incurs the danger of excessive abstraction and transcendence and loss of self, the horizontal search incurs the danger of entrapment in immanence. Binx may become so absorbed in the particularities of experience that he loses sight of their connectedness to the whole order of reality. In short, he forgets to muse. Musement, Peirce argued, is a fallible process of reasoning, and the muser can become seduced by his own self-indulgence to the point of despair and thus forsake his vocation as muser. Binx recognizes this when he first defines the search:

> What is the nature of the search? you ask. Really it is very simple, at least for a fellow like me: so simple that it is easily overlooked.
>
> The search is what anyone would undertake if he were not sunk in the everydayness of his own life. This morning, for example, I felt as if I had come to myself on a strange island. And what does a castaway do? Why, he pokes around the neighborhood and he doesn't miss a trick.
>
> To become aware of the possibility of the search is to be onto something. Not to be onto something is to be in despair. (MG, 13)

Binx does not say, however, what the "something" is the searcher is to be "onto." While Peirce claimed that musement would lead inevitably to the idea of God, Binx knows that in his world even that idea has been so rationalized, so stripped of mystery, that the words no longer signify the reality. Binx's laconic reflection on the search points to this situation:

> What do you seek—God? you ask with a smile. I hesitate to answer, since all other Americans have settled the matter for themselves and to give such an answer would amount to setting myself a goal which everyone else has reached—and therefore raising a question in which no one has the slightest interest. Who wants to be dead last among one hundred and eighty million Americans? For, as everyone knows, the polls report that 98% of Americans believe in God and the remaining 2% are atheists and agnostics—which leaves not a single percentage point for a seeker. (13-14)

Here, Binx cleverly deflects the issue of his own belief in God, but he does not abandon his search, his musing. The "idea of God" comes back to him at crucial points in the novel, informing his quest, and as we see later, it is a decisive factor in the life choices he makes near the end of the novel.

Binx's ultimate reconciliation of vertical and horizontal searching, of God and science, of musing and a specific career, centers on three crucial relationships: with Kate Cutrer, with his father, and with the Jews. Each bears examination in some detail.

Beyond his self-indulgent lapses from the search, Binx's inability to integrate the life of a muser with a specific vocation is complicated by the fact that the idea of the search seems almost incommunicable. When he tries to speak of it to his cousin Kate, she tends to objectify it, robbing it of its free and open character, its mystery. After she and Binx attend a movie at a theatre Binx used to frequent, she tries to get him to define the search. When she asks if their movie-going is "part of the search," he says:

> I do not answer. She can only believe I am serious in her own fashion of being serious: as an antic sort of seriousness, which is not seriousness at all but despair masking as seriousness. I would as soon not speak to her of such things, since she is bound to understand it as a cultivated eccentricity. . . . (81-82)

Though mildly irritated with Kate, Binx nevertheless tries to explain, but significantly, he speaks only of the vertical search here.

> "If you walk in the front door of the laboratory, you undertake the vertical search. You have a specimen, a cubic centimeter of water or a frog or a pinch of salt or a star."
> "One learns general things?"
> "And there is excitement to the search."
> "Why?" she asks.
> "Because as you get deeper into the search, you unify. You understand more and more specimens by fewer and fewer formulae. There is the excitement. Of course you are always after the big one, the new key, the secret leverage point, and that is the best of it."
> "And it doesn't matter where you are or who you are."
> "No."
> "And the danger is of becoming no one nowhere."
> "Never mind."
> Kate parses it out with the keen male bent of her mind, and yet with her woman's despair. Therefore I take care to be no more serious than she.
> "On the other hand, if you sit back here and take a little carcass out of the garbage can, a specimen which has been used and discarded, there remains something left over, a clue?"
> "Yes, but let's go."
> "You're a cold one, dear."
> "As cold as you?"
> "Colder. Cold as the grave." She walks about tearing shreds of flesh from her thumb. I say nothing. It would take very little to set her off on an attack on me, one of her "frank" appraisals. "It is possible, you know, that you are overlooking something, the most obvious thing of all. And you would not know it if you fell over it."
> "What?"
> She will not tell me. (82-83)

In this conversation, Percy probes to the core of Binx's dilemma over his search. When Kate takes up Binx's definition of the vertical search and says that there is something "left over," a "clue," after the specimen has been discarded, she is parroting Binx's own sense of the inadequacy of the scientific search. Like him, she senses that there is more to the *real* event than analyzing specimen and abstracting knowledge.

However, Binx shies away from Kate's probing. He fears that she is trying to rationalize the meaning of the search since she is prone to objectifying experience. But in his refusal to continue a "searching" conversation with Kate, Binx himself dichotomizes her in his mind—"keen male bent of her mind" and "female despair"—and so abandons seriousness. He fears one of her "frank appraisals."

The significance of Binx's "refusal" of Kate here is important for understanding his development. Communication between them is itself a triadic event, one in which they begin to *name* together the meaning of Binx's searches. (It is obvious from their conversation that he has tried to share his notions of vertical and horizontal searches with her before.) Their communion itself exemplifies a horizontal search, based on love and shared intimacy. Binx abandons *this* search here on the grounds that he is wary of Kate's problems. He also recognizes, correctly, that Kate's "seriousness" tends to undermine the freedom and play which is at the heart of successful musing, by moving toward objective closure. Yet while Binx's insights about her may be correct he is also unwilling to commit himself fully to Kate at this point, to accept her *as she is*. By the end of the novel Binx does come to make such a commitment, just as he commits himself to a career in medicine. In other words, Percy suggests a solution to the dilemma that the two searches pose for Binx: to search *with* another—in love—and to be "for others" in a practical way. To be, in other words, a searcher and a healer rather than merely a re-searcher.

A second major clue to the meaning of Binx's search is to be found in his growing understanding of his physician father. "Any doings of my father, even his signature, is in the nature of a clue in my search" (71). Although his father died an heroic death in World War II, crashing into the "wine-dark sea" off Crete, Binx guesses that his death was really a suicidal confirmation of his despair. Binx's mother, Mrs. Smith, claims that his father's "trouble" was that he was "overwrought," temperamentally unfit to be an ordinary physician and more suited for research (154). But Binx sees his father as the victim of a deeper despair that was only relieved by the catastrophe of war. Like his son, the elder Binx was a searcher and a muser, but one saturated with the spirit of scientism. Before the war, his searchings had led him to a point where even eating did not matter to him. He had reached the nil-point of feeling as "left-over" and canceled out from his search as Binx felt in the Birmingham hotel. Binx shares a good deal of his father's disposition, but he knows more about his predicament, especially about how the vertical search is an escape from the self. He says "That's what killed my father, English romanticism, that and 1930 science. A line from my notebook:

> 'Explore connection between romanticism and scientific
> objectivity. Does a scientifically minded person become
> a romantic because he is left over from his own sci-
> ence?'" (88)

Binx relates his father's ennui—the sense that nothing is worth doing—to himself when he tries to explain to his mother both his and his father's apparent lack of interest in ordinary life. Discussing his father's supposed "laziness," Binx tells his mother: "It is not laziness, Mother. Partly but not all" (157). Trying to explain, Binx recounts an experience during the Korean War when he fell asleep at a crossroad while waiting to inform the remnant of a Ranger company about a change in the plan of retreat. Binx fails to alert them, and the remnant is subsequently destroyed. His mother assumes that Binx is trying now to explain the horrible trauma of the experience, but Binx says: "That wasn't it. For a long time I couldn't remember anything. All I knew was that something was terribly wrong." The something "terribly wrong," Binx says, was not his part in the death of the soldiers.

> "It was not my conscience that bothered me. What I am
> trying to tell you is that nothing seemed worth doing
> except something I couldn't even remember. If somebody
> had come up to me and said: 'If you will forget your pre-
> occupations for forty minutes and get to work, I can as-
> sure you that you will find the cure of cancer and com-
> pose the greatest of all symphonies'—I wouldn't have
> been interested. Do you know why? Because it wasn't
> good enough for me."
> "That's selfish."
> "I know." (158)

Mrs. Smith's charge that Binx is selfish, and his apparent agreement, is too simplistic to explain his situation. In one sense it is true that Binx's lack of interest in curing cancer or writing the greatest symphony is a mark of his subtle pride—his secret egoistic sense that such discoveries or creations aren't good enough for him. But on a deeper level Binx's lack of interest is correct, because he knows that such achievements, important as they are, do not solve the ultimate mysteries of which the real search is the object; i.e. the mystery of God and the meaning of human existence. Binx is selfish only insofar that he is the only "self" who can undertake this search for himself. No one else can do it for him. And as he says later, he will help others "for good and selfish reasons"; that is, he will give himself unselfishly to others for the sake of his own soul.

Binx knows that his father shared the same "selfish" concern, knows that the clues he can find in his father's failed search are crucial to his own dilemmas. His father's search failed because, saturated with the spirit of scientism and without reference to God, his musings degenerated into feckless romanticism, leaving him feeling "left over" from his science until the war provided him with the chance for stoical, sacrificial death.

But unlike his father, Binx vows *not* to be defeated by everydayness, a vow linked explicitly to a search kept open to the possibility of God. Awakening at the Smith's summer house, Binx reports a series of crucial recognitions:

> Everydayness is the enemy. No search is possible. Perhaps there was a time when everydayness was not too strong and one could break its grip by brute strength. Now nothing breaks it—but disaster. Only once in my life was the grip of everydayness broken: when I lay bleeding in a ditch.
> . . . Nevertheless I vow: I'm a son of a bitch if I'll be defeated by everydayness.
> REMEMBER TOMORROW
> Starting point for the search:
> It no longer avails to start with creatures and prove God.
> Yet it is impossible to rule God out.
> The only possible starting point: the strange fact of one's own invincible apathy—that if the proofs were proved and God presented himself, nothing would be changed. Here is the strangest fact of all. Abraham saw signs and believed. Now the only sign is that all the signs in the world make no difference. Is this God's ironic revenge. *But I am onto Him.* (146) (My italics)

Binx believes that the traditional signs of God have become bankrupt or canceled out in the 20th century. This "loss " of God is a semiotic breakdown. Nevertheless, Binx does not relinquish the possibility of God's reality and His presence in the world. In his musings he keeps returning to some "vague" but real notion of God, as Peirce claimed the muser would. Thus Binx vows to continue to search for the God he is "onto."

Binx's recognition of the failure of his father, and his new awakening to the search, lead him to his most important clue— his kinship with the Jews.

> Ever since Wednesday I have become acutely aware of Jews. There is a clue here, but of what I cannot say . . . it is true that I am Jewish by instinct. We share the same exile. The fact is, however, I am more Jewish than the Jews I know. They are more at home than I am . . . Jews are my first real clue.
>
> When a man is in despair and does not in his heart of hearts allow that a search is possible and when such a man passes a Jew in the streets, he notices nothing. When a man becomes a scientist or an artist, he is open to a different kind of despair. When such a man passes a Jew in the street, he may notice something but it is not a remarkable encounter. To him the Jew can only appear as a scientist or artist like himself or as specimen to be studied.
>
> But when a man awakens to the possibility of a search and when such a man passes a Jew in the street for the first time, he is like Robinson Crusoe seeing the footprint on the beach. (88-89)

This speech indicates a crucial turning point in Binx's journey as a muser. First of all, Percy's allusion to the scientist and the artist is no accident. In Binx's later musing on the dilemmas of searching he specifically mentioned science (the cure for cancer) and art (the composer) as examples of transcendence of reality that he would reject as "not good enough" for him. He believes such achievements ultimately lead to despair for the self; they are unable to solve the transcendence-immanence split that was his father's doom. Percy later made the same point about the scientist and the artist in *Lost in the Cosmos* (141-167). But now Binx senses that somehow the Jews are a sign of how that split might be resolved. For Binx the Jews are a sign of how one might exist, albeit as an exile, in a world that is at one and the same time both itself and yet somehow transfigured in meaning.

As is well known Percy argued in several essays and in *The Thanatos Syndrome* that the meaning of the Jews is at the center of the "Judeo-Christian Event" in history, God's communication of Himself to the Hebrews as His chosen people, and His subsequent entrance into history in the person of Jesus Christ. The "Jewish-Christian Event," as Percy called it, becomes the axis of history, the point of intersection for the immanent and transcendent, the divine and the mundane, and time and the eternal. This event is a semiotic event, a communication of divine being; the Jews themselves are therefore a sign of God's presence in the world, and because of their unique historical particularity they cannot be abstracted into a category. As Fr. Smith says in *The Thanatos Syndrome*: "The Jews as a word sign cannot be assimilated under a class, category, or theory. No subsuming Jews!"[9] Moreover, because of the Judeo-Christian event, ordinary commonplace reality is transformed and given absolute value in the eternal. Everything matters, and everything counts. Therefore, since the Jews are a central clue in Binx's search, and since to muse is to search, then they are a clue to *the way* Binx must journey through the world. The Judeo-Christian event gives special meaning, purpose and direction to history and how to act within history. We recalled how Peirce maintained that musement would not only lead the muser to a consideration of the reality of God, but also lead *practically* to an ethical commitment in the world, since musement about God is a force influencing "the whole conduct of life." Therefore, through his musings about the God he is "on to," and about the Jews as the principle clue to its meaning, Binx is led to choose a new life, a vocation, and a career. In marrying Kate Cutrer and entering medical school, Binx can continue to live as a muser—still searching for God amidst His earthly signs—and unite that search with the practical, specific vocation of physician-healer of others. Just as Kate needs Binx's care, so also does Binx need Kate's love to save him from solipsism, from a life of romantic longing for transcendence, and from despair. With her and in his career as physician, he is free to become a man for others.

In the epilogue of the novel, although Binx refuses to speak of his search, he has clearly not abandoned it. Earlier, when Kate asks him what he plans to do, Binx announces his vocation:

> There is only one thing to do: listen to people, see how they stick themselves into the world, hand them along in their dark journey and be handed along, and for good and selfish reasons. It remains only to decide whether this vocation is best pursued in a service station or. . . .
> (233)

As the passage suggests, the external form—a career—is not so important to Binx as his inner vocation, a physician being another form of "service" to others. And, I would argue, the religious and moral foundation of that vocation is his life as a

muser. One sign of Binx's continued practice of the life of religious muser is revealed when he sees a black man leaving a
church on Ash Wednesday. As the man passes, Binx muses
about the meaning of the event.

> I watch him closely in the rear-view mirror. It is im-
> possible to say why he is here. Is it part and parcel of
> the complex business of coming up in the world? Or is it
> because he believes God is present here at the corner of
> Elysian Fields and Bons Enfants? Or is he here for both
> reasons: through some dim, dazzling gift of grace, com-
> ing for the one and receiving the other as God's own im-
> portuante bonus?
> It is impossible to say. (234-235)

Here, Binx remains open as a muser to the mystery of the event,
the enigma of the signs, acknowledging the possibility of the
confluence of the divine and the mundane ordinary world,
aware that though he may be "onto" God, nevertheless as Peirce
said the idea is always shrouded in "vagueness" and cannot be
explained in human language. "It is impossible to say."

Yet Binx's continuing musement is rooted in a belief in
the Judeo-Christian Event. When the Smith children ask Binx
whether at the final resurrection their brother Lonnie will be
like them, restored completely whole in body and spirit, he answers "yes," an affirmation which Percy considered one of the
most important "clues" to the meaning of the novel.[10] In this
remark Binx affirms the resurrection as the culmination of the
Judeo-Christian event, the final triumphant transfiguration of
human history.

By the end of the novel, Binx has begun to learn to combine the vertical and horizontal searches, to be a doctor and a
man for others, and yet one who freely keeps his gaze on "the
collective total of all that is in any sense present to the mind"—
Binx Bolling, musing scientist.

Notes

[1] Walker Percy. *The Moviegoer*. New York: Alfred A. Knopf, 1961.
Noonday Press edition, 1967, pp. 51-52. Hereafter cited in the text.
    [2] Walker Percy. *Lost in the Cosmos*. New York: Farrar, Straus and
Giroux, 1983, pp. 160-167. Hereafter cited in the text as *Cosmos*.

[3] See "The Fateful Rift: The San Andreas Fault in the Modern Mind," in *Signposts in a Strange Land*, Patrick Samway, S.J., ed. New York: Farrar, Straus and Giroux, 1991, pp. 271-291.

[4] References to Peirce's semiotic theories abound in Percy's writings and are well known. However, a systematic study of the development of Peirce's influence on Percy's thought has not as yet, to my knowledge, been undertaken. Nevertheless, Percy's essay "Semiotic and a Theory of Knowledge" reveals his familiarity with Peirce's thought early in his career. This essay first appeared in *Modern Schoolman*, 34 (1957): 225-246, four years prior to the publication of *The Moviegoer*.

[5] See especially "Why Are You A Catholic?", pp. 304-315, "Culture, the Church, and Evangelization," pp. 295-303, and "Another Message in the Bottle," pp. 352-367, in *Signposts*.

[6] *Collected Papers of Charles Sanders Peirce*. Charles Hartshorne and Paul Weiss, ed. Cambridge: Belknap Press of Harvard Press, 1935, 1958. References by volume and paragraph number: read "CP. 6. 488" as Vol. 6, para. 488. All further references cited in the text.

[7] Walker Percy. *The Message in the Bottle*. New York: Farrar, Straus and Giroux, 1975, p. 321. Hereafter cited in the text.

[8] Peirce's allusion here to three "Universes" is a reference to his three primal ontological categories—firstness, secondness, and thirdness—that form the basis of his semiotic. For a fuller discussion of this theory, see Chap. 3 of Robert S. Corrington's *An Introduction to C. S. Peirce*, Lanham, MD: Rowan and Littlefield, Publishers, Inc., 1933, pp. 117-166.

[9] Walker Percy. *The Thanatos Syndrome*. New York: Farrar, Straus and Giroux, 1987, p. 126.

[10] Lawson, Lewis and Victor A. Kramer, ed. *More Conversations with Walker Percy*. Jackson: University of Mississippi, 1993, p. 146.

Walker Percy and T. S. Eliot—
The Lancelot Andrewes Connection

Walker Percy's importance as a 20th century writer rests not so much upon his Southern roots as on his place within a larger tradition of prophetic writers whose visions of the disarray in modern Western civilization have been a formidable challenge to our times. Along with many of his interpreters, Percy himself has acknowledged his allegiance to this tradition, the tradition of Kierkegaard and Dostoevsky, of Camus and Solezynitzyn, of T. S. Eliot, Thomas Merton and Flannery O'Connor. The roots of this tradition are ancient and most conspicuously, biblical, but in modern literature, the prophetic role of the writer has been particularly complicated by the fact that modern man's spiritual predicament is inextricably bound up with the problem of human self-consciousness, the self reflecting upon itself as a creature of history who nevertheless longs for authentic transcendence. Given this complication, it is not surprising that we should find a confluence of thought, image pattern, and artistic strategy between the poetry of T. S. Eliot and the fiction of Walker Percy. The prophetic vision is the light that shines strongly in both writers, and perhaps nowhere more strongly than in their profound dramatic monologues on the problems of the self-conscious self and its relationship to history: Eliot's "Gerontion" (1920) and Percy's *Lancelot* (1977).

Eliot's poem is a meditation on the corrupt state of modern Western culture delivered by an old man who is both witness to and victim of history. Percy's novel is a meditation by one Lancelot Lamar—Southern lawyer, owner of a baronial mansion called Belle Isle, married to a rich, lusty Texas girl named Margot. Their life together has become serenely sterile; in her restlessness Margot has turned to acting, her latest venture being to turn Belle Isle into a movie set and people the mansion with all manner of decadent Hollywood types. Lance

accepts this passively until he discovers Margot's infidelity with
her movie producer-directors Merlin and Jacoby, whereupon he
plots his revenge: to prove Margot's adultery and murder her
current lover. In the final catastrophic explosion the entire en-
tourage of movie people is killed, Belle Isle is destroyed, and
Lance survives after trying vainly to "save" his wife.

When the novel opens Lance is undergoing treatment at a
psychiatric clinic in New Orleans. Soon to be released, he plans
to marry the rape victim Anna and found a new society in Virginia. Lance's only visitor is his old friend Percival, a Catholic
priest who failed as a missionary in Uganda and now serves as
priest-physician (and patient?) at the clinic. The substance of the
novel is Lance's "confession" to Percival of what happened at
Belle Isle, his moral condemnation of contemporary society, and
his future plan for a new society in Virginia. Lance's monologue, as we shall see, has a strong spiritual affinity with that of
Eliot's seer Gerontion. But in the last analysis, Eliot and Percy
take divergent paths in their depiction of modern spiritual history, a divergence most clearly signified by their mutual use of
the Lancelot Andrewes connection.

One can begin by noting some rather remarkable parallels
between Eliot's poem and Percy's novel, parallels which, coinci-
dence or provable influence notwithstanding, lead I think to a
recognition of more substantive issues linking the two works.
These issues have to do with the very nature of modern consciousness, its dilemmas, and the meaning of action itself.

Both "Gerontion" and *Lancelot* use as their central image
the decaying house as emblems of Western civilization, last bas-
tion of the spirit of secularism and scientific humanism. Both
works dramatize the apocalyptic destruction of this world:
Gerontion envisions a cataclysmic unleashing of natural forces
at the end of the poem, where everything is "whirled/beyond
the circuit of the shuddering Bear/In fractured atoms . . ." (11. 67-
69); Lance's house is destroyed in a holocaust of perversion and
murder during a hurricane. The name of Lance's estate, "Belle
Isle," not only ironically evokes both the Camelot-esque ideal of
a perfect Christian social order and the blessed isle of the dead
heroes; it also echoes the concluding *topas* in Eliot's poem:
". . . the windy straits of Belle Isle." Gerontion lives in a world of
"Rock, moss, stone crop, iron, merde"; Lancelot's world is one of
bayous, oil wells, fake plantation memorabilia, technological
gimmickry, and "pigeon shit." In short, the worlds of these two

prophets are substantially alike. In addition, both works reveal the spiritual death that comes from a pursuit of sensual gratification. Lancelot complains of being "cold" and of deadened feelings near the end of the novel; Gerontion laments "I have lost my passion . . ," and knows himself as one who has been reduced to consciousness alone, "a dull head among windy spaces." More importantly, Percy's hero was named by his father for Lancelot Andrewes, the Anglican divine Eliot admired and whose sermons exerted profound influence on his poetry, including of course direct references in "Gerontion." Lance claims to have repudiated his namesake, but as I hope to show, the ideal society he plans to create in Virginia bears strong resemblance to that image of a Christian social order and culture which Eliot found so compellingly represented in Lancelot Andrewes's sermons, and the loss of which he adumbrates ironically in "Gerontion." But Percy finally rejects the possibility that this ideal of Christian society can be realized in history, precisely because such an idea is *only* historical. In fact, in Lance's plan Percy shows that any wedding of the notion of an ideal spiritual order to history is not only bound to fail, but that it intensifies modern spiritual malaise. It is in this respect that his vision diverges most radically from that of Eliot.

While "Gerontion" and *Lancelot* share a mutual vision of the modern self's relationship to history, they also share an affinity in their brilliant methods of dramatic presentation. In Eliot's poem, Gerontion assumes the role of prophet in the decadent house of modern civilization. This decadent condition, he infers, is due substantially to Western culture's defection from Christ, the "word within a word, unable to speak a word, swaddled in darkness." This defection constitutes a wrong turn in history, a turning away from a sacramental vision of reality in favor of secular knowledge and power, so that now history has become a dark labyrinth of "cunning passages" and "contrived corridors," a "wilderness of mirrors" that issues only in "vanities." But in Eliot's brilliant handling of the monologue, this dark labyrinth is also an image of the enclosed modern consciousness, a mind which has become totally identified with the secular historical process. The result of this identification, as Gerontion well knows, is ultimately sterile; secular knowledge without transcendent faith is incapable of sustaining the life of the spirit. "After such knowledge, what forgiveness?"

But as several critics of the poem have noted, Gerontion's self-appointed role as prophet is rendered suspect by the very form of the poem.[1] Gerontion's monologue may indeed be a confession of modern spiritual anomie, but it is also an elaborate self-justification for his own *acedia* and his unwillingness either to act in or take responsibility for history. Consequently, his prophesy of the coming apocalypse when "the tiger springs in the new year" becomes in fact a defense of his own passivity. (Whether this is unwitting self-delusion or a calculated "show" on Gerontion's part is impossible to ascertain fully, given the oblique method of dramatization. Nevertheless, that very insolubility is itself a manifestation of the predicament of self-consciousness.) Gerontion's "stance" toward history, then, is stoical, deterministic, and dissociated—the condition of gnosis—a stoicism which, as Hugh Kenner has noted, is the reverse of Christian humility. Gerontion, in fact, damns himself out of his own mouth (as Percy's Lancelot will also): the sterile, would-be seer therefore becomes identified with those false diviners in Dante's *Inferno* who presumed to tell the future. Although he pleads that this is a true revelation, he protests too much. Trapped within the spiritual dilemmas of his own times, Gerontion can only prophesy the natural devolution of history to a cataclysmic end. The only "escape" from this process of devolution, as Gerontion recognizes, would be through some transfiguring grace. But he denies the possibility of sacramental action; indeed, he bemoans its loss: "I that was near your heart was removed therefrom/to lose beauty in terror, terror in inquisition" (55-56). Most significantly, the very means of sacramental action, the physical senses, have become moribund in Gerontion. "I have lost my sight, smell, hearing, taste and touch: How should I use them for your closer contact?" (59-60).

Eliot's technique in "Gerontion" brilliantly manifests a use of reflexiveness that is perfectly coincident with the themes of the poem. The dramatic monologue enacts—with its abstract language, elliptical phrasing, broken lines, and circuitous arguments—the very condition of gnosis that Gerontion is describing. But Eliot dramatizes it in such a way that we as readers are able to grasp the larger perspective through which Gerontion's flawed vision can be named and judged. We note the partiality in his vision of history, and the self-exculpating tendency of his own mind. Like Percy's Lancelot, Gerontion sees the evils of his times, but not his own weakness; his acknowledgement of per-

sonal failure is so thoroughly diffused as part of the general situation that it really absolves him of responsibility. Self-pity replaces true *metanoia*; historical situation becomes Gerontion's
excuse for inaction as he projects himself as a passive victim of
circumstances ("I was neither at the hot gates/Nor fought in
warm rain . . ." (3-4).

But historical circumstances also belie his protest. Eliot
implicitly measures the distortion in Gerontion's view of the
self in history by evoking the Christian sacramental vision of reality, a belief which Gerontion feels is now lost, replaced by the
decadent rituals of Mr. Silvero, Hakagawa, Madame de Tourn-
quist, and Fraulein von Kulp. Their new sacramentals are the
occult trappings of a culture in which idolatry and superstition
have replaced religion. Their rituals are signs emptied of transcendent significance, cut off from the source of mystery, the divine Logos. Small wonder that in such an age the Word should
be "swaddled in darkness"—and that both Eliot and Percy would
choose as formal strategy a representing of this numinous
"silence," Eliot by his oblique evocation of the sacramental vision, and Percy by the use of his "silent" witness/listener, Percival. In both works, protagonist and reader alike must piece out
the transforming sacramental vision from the shards of broken
signs that bombard the modern consciousness, much as Lancelot
has to piece together the meaning of the half-visible sign outside
his cell window in the opening of the novel.

Just as powerfully as Eliot's poem, Percy's novel depicts
the devaluation of a sacramental vision of reality and the
dilemmas of modern self-consciousness in relation to history.
Gerontion's passive, unheroic posture throughout the poem is
echoed in Lancelot's spiritual torpor before his discovery of Margot's adultery. Lance also laments the lost possibility of heroic
action, which he believes existed in his forefathers. His lament
takes the form of a romantic obsession with a gnostic ideal of
heroic action, an ideal which seemingly collapsed for Lance
when he discovered his father's thievery and moral cowardice.
That this sense of bankruptcy should issue from the novel's pu-
tative representative of *via media* Anglicanism, that version of
"Christendom" as cultural entity described with admiration by
Eliot in his essay on Lancelot Andrewes, is not without significance, as we shall see. Nevertheless, as Percy makes clear,
Lance's gnostic ideal still lives in memory, an unrecognized obsession ready to be actuated under the right circumstances. Thus

Lance's ideal of action will lead him finally to sadism and murder.

Before his discovery of Margot's infidelity, Lance has performed acknowledged "good" acts—his work as a lawyer in the
Civil Rights movement, for example—but even these acts are
hollow to him, "virtues . . . forced upon us by our impudent
crimes . . ," as Gerontion would say. In Lance's world of Belle
Isle the sacramental vision has been lost, and with its loss the
transcendent significance of action has also apparently collapsed.
Consequently, there is a "logical" connection between this collapse and Lance's unholy quest to revive the heroic act in purely
secular terms, for the discovery of Margot's adultery sends him
on a quest for the mystery of evil as embodied in that most mysterious of human acts—sex. But given his gnostic mentality and
mechanistic conception of action, Lance's quest can only issue in
failure. The so-called "discovery" Lance makes about the sex act
and murder is that it is only a matter of molecular rearrange-
ment. They are acts which, *pace* Gerontion, merely "excite the
membrane," performed in a world governed completely by biological and mechanical forces, a world of "fractured atoms."
What could be more Gerontion-esque that Lance's self-justifying
description of the failure of his quest?

> The question is: Why did I discover nothing at the
> heart of evil? There was no 'secret' after all, not even
> any evil. There was no sense of coming close to the 'an-
> swer' as there had been when I discovered the stolen
> money in my father's sock drawer. As I held the
> wretched Jacoby by the throat, I felt nothing except the
> itch of fiberglass particles under my collar.[2]

Gerontion's world of decadent rituals and corrupted
sacramentals has "advanced" in Percy's novel to the new sacramentals of secular knowledge—technological gimmickry.
Lance's house becomes a movie set given over to factitious imi-
tations of nature, and the instruments of his own demonic quest
are the tools of dissociated power: cameras, voice and video tape
recorders and technological know-how. At the control of this
electronic wizardry sits Lancelot, the dissociated rational self
who, like Gerontion, has assumed the role of *voyeur* to history's
cunning turns and deceptions. Lance even creates his own
"wilderness of mirrors," literally, to trap Margot and her lover at
the motel. And all the while from his God-like stance of *voyeur*
Lance presumes to judge the actions of others and exact cruel
vengence. "After such knowledge, what forgiveness?" Yet like

Gerontion, he fails to acknowledge his own responsibility for history—his sexual exploitation of Margot preceding her adultery, for example—so the only knowledge Lance gleans from his quest is the recognition, like Gerontion's, of his own spiritual sterility.

> . . . You know the feeling of numbness and coldness, no, not a feeling, but a lack of feeling, that I spoke of during the events at Belle Isle? I told you it might have been the effect of the hurricane, the low pressure, methane, whatever. But I still feel it. That is, today, I don't feel it. I don't feel anything—except a slight curiosity about walking down that street out there. (274)

Percy's technique in dramatizing Lance's predicament is no less ingenious than Eliot's and may indeed owe something to it. Lance's monologue is part prophesy, part confession and part rationalization. He assumes the role of dire prophet to reveal the age's corruption, but his monologue is also an elaborate self-deception. Like Gerontion, he embodies the situation of the mind closed within history, saturated with knowledge but devoid of faith. Both figures are obsessed with the meaning of history, and though Lance tries to dismiss the past as banal and "feckless," his entire monologue is in fact a meditation on the past and its significance. Lance appears to have moved beyond the spiritual inertia of Gerontion insofar that he *does* act, but his actions are either damning and sterile (his murderous revenge) or so inhumanely gnostic as to constitute an escape from history (his plan for a new Eden in Virginia). His confession, then, is in this regard as much a "show" and "concitation of the backward devils" as Gerontion's is.

But there are crucial differences between Gerontion and Lancelot as self-appointed prophets, differences that concern the religious vision that informs the two works. One notes, initially, the more palpable sense of hope in *Lancelot*. True, in "Gerontion" the old man is "waiting for rain," Eliot's sign of spiritual revitalization. It may also be, as some have argued, that Gerontion's confession, though tainted with self-justification, is nevertheless an incipient sign of possible conversion, a kind of *via negitiva* which may bring him to true penance. But hope is muted in Eliot's poem. Gerontion is still the "dull head among windy spaces" at the end of the poem, a Prufrockian equivocator unwilling to act.

In *Lancelot*, the potential for disaster has magnified over Gerontion's world, but so has the possibility of hope, incarnated in the novel in the figure of the "silent" confessor Percival/ Father John. Unlike Gerontion, Lance does act, albeit in unholy fashion. He has committed murder and acts of sexual sadism. But in addition to his overt actions, Lance's long conversation with Percival constitutes an important act of memory in which his self-justifying arguments are exposed as a failure: Anna the rape victim will not become the idealized woman of his new Eden, and Percival completely rejects Lance's gnostic interpretation of history. Percival himself has undergone his own process of spiritual healing. *His* plan of action at the end of the novel points a way out of the dilemmas posed by Lance's situation. Instead of going to proselytize Africans, Percival will minister to common, middle-class parishoners in a small parish in Alabama. The penitential way replaces the heroic quest. Percival will live humbly in the fallen world and accept its fallenness. Most importantly, he will administer the sacraments to a congregation of believers. So the sacramental vision lives in Percy's novel as a vital force, whereas Gerontion recalls it only as something lost or rendered meaningless ". . . if still believed/In memory only, reconsidered passion . . ," or debased into superstition:

> In depraved May, dogwood and chestnut, flowering judas,
> To be eaten, to be divided, to be drunk
> Among whispers; by Mr. Silvero
> With caressing hands, at Limoges
> Who walked all night in the next room;
>
> By Hakagawa, bowing among the Titians;
> By Madame de Tournquist, in the dark room
> Shifting the candles. . . . (21-28)

The change which occurs in Percival, indicated by his resuming priestly garb in the novel, is a clear sign of the possibility of *metanoia*, and as the novel ends, it is Percival who now has something to say to Lance. As confessor-therapist, he has adroitly led Lance to admit the emptiness of his actions, and to begin to glimpse that the source of his *acedia* is the absence in him of redeeming love.

But are the significant differences in the religious visions which inform the two remarkably similar works simply due to differences in temperment between Eliot and Percy? Or is it because Percy is a latter day prophetic writer, one who has the "advantage" of having witnessed more recent cataclysms both outside of and within the human consciousness, thus making his vision more extreme? Possibly. But there is hardly an aspect of the contemporary spiritual malaise which had not already been foreseen prophetically in Eliot's work. The difference, it seems to me, is bound up with the question of the meaning of history projected in the two works, and is signified by the different attitudes of Eliot and Percy toward Lancelot Andrewes.

Eliot's unbounded admiration for Andrewes as a preacher, particularly for his sermons on the Incarnation, is intimately bound up with his view of Andrewes's central role in helping to construct the Anglican Church's *via media* stance between the extremes of papacy and presbytery. For Eliot, this stance reflects his own view of the relationship between church polity, history, and culture. After proclaiming the "*via media* which is the spirit of Anglicanism . . ," Eliot enlarges the theme:

> . . . a Church is to be judged by its intellectual fruits, by its influence on the sensibility of the most sensitive and on the intellect of the most intelligent, and it must be made real to the eye by monuments of artistic merit.[3]
>
> . . . .
>
> No religion can survive the judgement of history unless the best minds of its time have collaborated in its construction; if the Church of Elizabeth is worthy of the age of Shakespeare and Jonson, that is because of the work of Hooker and Andrewes. (291)

Two significant aspects of Eliot's statement stand out in relation to any comparison one wishes to make between his religious vision and Percy's. The first is Eliot's argument that a Church be judged by its "intellectual fruits" and "monuments of artistic merit" which "must be made real to the eye. . . ." Such a view reveals a crucial shift in emphasis—away from the traditional signs and sources of Christianity's vitality: the sacraments, which are "real to the eye" as physical signs of transcendent mysteries—and towards an emphasis upon cultural artifacts, artistic and intellectual fruits, as the mark of the Church's vitality. The second significant aspect of Eliot's statement derives from this shift in emphasis, and that is that his statement betokens a view of Church polity as inextricably wedded to culture and history. In short, it views the church fundamentally as an historical entity, and the traditional tension between Christianity's historical and eschatalogical identity—a tension incarnated in the sacraments—is effectively vitiated. Eliot's view strongly suggests that

identification of Christianity and culture which Kierkegaard dis-
paragingly branded as "Christendom," the church vitiated by its
absorption within historicism, and against which Kierkegaard
posed a radically existential and mysterious Christianity.

Just as Eliot understands Anglicanism as an image of order in human history—a *via media*—so also does he understand
Andrewes's sermons as literary manifestations of pre-modern
unity within the Western personality, a harmony which is
particularly expressed in the poetic temperment. Regarding
Andrewes's style, Eliot notes that ". . . his passion for order in religion is reflected in his passion for order in prose" (294). The
conspicuous qualities of this style are "ordonnance, or arrange-
ment and structure, and relevant intensity," made possible by
the harmony of sensibility and intellect Eliot finds in Andrewes
that gives his prose a "purity" lacking in his more popular contemporary, John Donne. Andrewes's "emotion is purely con-
templative; it is not personal, it is wholly evoked by the object of
contemplation, to which it is adequate; his emotions wholly
contained in and explained by its object" (298-299). For Eliot,
Andrewes is the "more medieval, because he is the more pure,
and because his bond was with the Church, with tradition . . .";
while Donne is "more modern," a writer of divided sensibility
whose sermons contain potentialities for indulgence in "personality" for its own sake and "a certain wantonness of the spirit."
While Eliot is careful to distinguish the two sermon writers
without prejudice, there is little doubt that he sees embodied in
Andrewes an ideal of the man of letters, theologian, and believer
whose *integritas* (wholeness) has not been shattered by the divi-
sive forces of modernity. And this integrity of spirit is especially
manifested in Andrewes' use of language.

> To persons whose minds are habituated to feed on the
> vague jargon of our time, when we have a vocabulary
> for everything and exact ideas about nothing—when a
> word half-understood, torn from its place in some alien
> or half-toned science, as of psychology, conceals from
> both writer and reader the meaninglessness of a state-
> ment, when all dogma is in doubt except the dogmas of
> science of which we have read in the newspapers, when
> the language of theology itself, under the influence of
> an undisciplined mysticism of popular philosophy,
> tends to become a language of tergiversation—
> Andrewes may seem pedantic and verbal. It is only
> when we have saturated ourselves in his prose, fol-
> lowed the movement of his thought, that we find his

> examination of words terminating in the ecstasy of as-
> sent. Andrewes takes a word and derives the world
> from it; squeezing and squeezing the word until it yields
> a full juice of meaning which we should never have
> supposed any word to possess. In this process the quali-
> ties which we have mentioned, of ordonnance and pre-
> cision, are exercised. (295)

The ideal of language expressed here is of course an incarnational one, of perfect correspondence between language and object, between word and act; hence Eliot's singling out of
Andrewes's seventeen sermons on the Nativity as particularly
exemplary of the Anglican's genius. In sum, Andrewes's sermons on the Incarnation display a faith in the redemptive
power of language itself which is obviously close to Eliot's own
heart as a poet. In "Gerontion," of course, Andrewes' very
phrasing is interpolated into the text of the poem—"The word
within a word, unable to speak a word/Swaddled with darkness"
(18-19).

In Gerontion's monologue we see that the vital spirituality keynoted by the Andrewes reference—"the word within a
word"—exists only as a memory in the mind of the would-be
prophet, a fading vision which is impotent against the mechanistic forces that govern history within the poem. Dissociation—the sundering of men's spirit—has for a few hundred
years been the condition of the modern self, and language itself
is a victim of this devisive, gnostic condition.[4] Hence Percival's
"silence" throughout most of the novel. As Percy said, the old
terms have "slipped their moorings"; the old words—particularly the received language of Christendom—have become as
devalued as old poker chips. But for the believer this slippage
has *no effect* whatsoever on the efficacy of the sacraments. In
the case of Gerontion, however, his lament for the loss of the
power of the Christian vision in history reflects Eliot's own
lament for the dissociation of language from the sacramental act
itself, since as I have already indicated, Eliot's view that the
Church's significance in history is based upon its intellectual and
artistic merits reveals a fatal shift away from the sacramental—
and hence trans-historical—source of Christianity's vitality. At
the same time, it also implicitly reflects Eliot's hope that the
Christian vision might be reconstituted within history, within
culture. But the dissociation between verbal sign and sacramental *action*—between logos and mystery—is nonetheless there,
and it may well account for his emphasis upon the qualities of

order and precision in Andrewes's language, rather than on numinosity and mystery. In the last analysis, there is no sacramental action for Gerontion; there is no way to bridge the gap between "the word within a word" and the decadent milieu of "cunning passages," "unnatural vices," "vanities," and "impudent crimes" he inhabits.

Percy's use of the Lancelot Andrewes connection is much more ironical, and it reveals the fundamental difference between his vision and Eliot's. In the novel the Lamars are Anglicans, unlike the Catholic Percival (and Percy). Lance has been named after the Anglican priest by his father, but his father is an ineffectual dreamer and "poet" given to lofty visions of quaint Anglican parishes throughout the South. His vision, in fact, is that of a *via media* Christendom wedded to an ideal of genteel, "honorable" society and culture. Lance recalls it with droll sarcasm: ". . . my father screwed up by poesy, dreaming of Robert E. Lee and Lancelot Andrewes and Episcopal chapels in the wildwood . . ." (57).

> My father: a failed man who missed the boat all around but who knew how far away Arcturus was. He was editor of a local weekly, where he published his own poems and historical vignettes about this region on such subjects as St. Andrew's Chapel: the first Non-Roman Church in the Parish. . . . The Kiwanas Club gave him a certificate officially entitling him the Poet Laureate of Feliciana Parish. He was an ordinary newspaper poet, and ordinary newspaper historian, and he had an ordinary newspaperman's wonder about science. (59)

While recognizing his father's ordinariness, Lance also perceives the romantically gnostic quality of his father's longings, especially the fact that his desire for a culture of Christendom governed by "quaint Anglican parishes" is a modern descendent of the ideal of a community of Christendom embodied in Arthurian legend. His father's ideal, in other words, strongly suggests that vision of Christendom in history articulated in the Protestant Reformation with its attempt to purify church and state, and the English form of this ideal of *via media* Christendom is for Eliot best represented by Lancelot Andrewes. Yet such a vision represents a tacit repudiation of history, a movement toward dissociation, and a dilution of the incarnational mystery that is at the center of the sacramental life. Although Lance does not recognize the implications in these terms (as Percival does), he does intuit the peculiar bankruptcy of this inheritance, especially when he reflects on his own naming. Commenting on his father's library, he observes:

> . . . a strange collection in which I could detect no common denominator except a taste for the extraordinary and marvelous, the sentimental, the extraordinary experience, the extraordinary adventure undertaken by a brave few, the extraordinary life of genius, the extraordinary glory of a lost cause which becomes more extraordinary as it recedes in time and in fact Robert E. Lee and the Army of Northern Virginia had long since become for him as legendary and mythical as King Arthur and the Round Table. Do you think I was named Lancelot for nothing? The Andrewes was tacked on by him to give it Episcopal sanction, but what he really had in mind and really wanted to be and couldn't have been more different from was that old nonexistent brawler and adulterer, Lancelot du Lac, King Ban of Benwick's son, knight of the Round Table and—here was the part he could never get over—one of only two knights to see the Grail (you, Percival, the other); and above all the extraordinariness of *those chaste and incorrupt* little Anglican chapels set down in this violent and corrupt land besieged on all sides by savage Indians, superstitious Romans, mealy-mouthed Baptists, howling Holy-Rollers. (122-123) (My italics)

Lance's father, a romantic longing for the "extraordinariness of those chaste and incorrupt little Anglican chapels," suffers from a fatal gnosticism which renders him ineffectual. Above all, his longing reveals an inability to see the extraordinary in the ordinary, which is precisely the mystery of the sacramental life that Percival finally represents.

But Lance himself is no more successful than his father at solving the dilemmas posed by his spiritual inheritance. Lance cannot forgive his father's "refusal" to act heroically and honorably. At the same time, he recognizes the spiritual bankruptcy inherent in the tradition of Christendom signified by his namesake. Lance repudiates this tradition and, unlike his father and Eliot's Gerontion, seemingly comes to act decisively. But to what end? Like Gerontion, Lance is a master of rhetoric, an eloquent critic of the spiritual ills of modern society. But to what purpose is this eloquent "show" of language? What we discover finally in Lance's monologue is the same fissure between word and act, the same dissociation between mind and external reality that dooms Gerontion. The reason is that Lance's plan to resurrect a heroic social order in Virginia is a modern, secular version of his father's dream of a society of honor and "quaint Anglican parishes," a dream of an achieved cultural ideal in history which, paradoxically, repudiates history. It is a society without sacraments, a society whose central premise is self-redemption through human means alone, a society in which love is cut off from the source of love.

But Percy does not give Lance the final word in the novel, as Eliot does Gerontion. Against Lance's gnosticism stands Percival, who will not speak the unspeakable mystery which cannot be spoken, but whose actions point the way to what both Gerontion and Lancelot have lost—the sacramental vision. For Percival, the choice is not between a *via media* Christendom rendered bankrupt by modernity and a new self-redeemed heroic social order that repudiates history. Percival instead chooses a Christianity which is not totally identified with history and culture, a Christianity whose historical character is balanced in the mysterious tension of its eschatalogical reality. And the specific locus of this tension is the sacrament itself—which is not simply sign or word, and thus historically conditioned, but is also an eschatalogical *event*, and therefore supra-historical. It is this mysterious power of sacrament—of transcendence *through* immanence—which is lacking in Gerontion and Lancelot. But Percival possesses this means of grace, so that he can enter history not in order to remake it in secular terms, but to direct it authentically toward its ultimate transfiguration.

Notes

[1] Especially relevant for this discussion of "Gerontion" are the following: Elizabeth Drew, *T. S. Eliot: The Design of His Poetry*. New York, 1949; and Hugh Kenner, *The Invisible Poet: T. S. Eliot*. New York, 1959.

[2] Walker Percy. *Lancelot*. New York: Avon Books, 1977, pp. 274-275. All further references are to this edition and are cited in the text.

[3] T. S. Eliot. "For Lancelot Andrewes," in *Selected Essays: 1917-1932*. New York: Harcourt, Brace & Co., 1932, p. 290. All further citations are from this edition and are cited in the text.

[4] The situation I describe here has been brilliantly discussed by Eric Voegelin in *The New Science of Politics*. Chicago: University of Chicago Press, 1952; and in *From Enlightenment To Revolution*. Durham, NC: Duke University Press, 1975. See also Cleanth Brooks' helpful essay, "Walker Percy and Modern

Gnosticism," in *The Art of Walker Percy*. Panthea Reid Broughton, ed. Baton Rouge and London: Louisiana State University Press, 1979, pp. 26-72.

From Suicide to Ex-Suicide:
Notes on the Southern Writer as Hero in the
Age of Despair

Throughout his career Walker Percy insisted on separating himself from the tradition of Southern letters represented by William Faulkner, a tradition he saw as concerned mainly with confronting the past through story-telling. In essays and interviews, Percy aligned himself instead with modern European writers, especially Dostoevsky, Sartre, and Camus. Percy's claimed interest was in the new South and its problems of technological transformation and spiritual dislocation, problems he saw not as regional but as endemic in all modern Western culture. Percy did, however, acknowledge one important point of contact with Faulkner—his interest in "a Quentin Compson who did not commit suicide."

> I'm kind of a maverick; that is, I don't fit in to the Southern pattern. All my characters, whether from Binx Bolling to Will Barrett to Thomas More and others, find themselves in the here-and-now predicament. And the whole backdrop is the historical scene which is drawn so well by Shelby (Foote), Eudora (Welty), and Faulkner. It's there, all right, but my character is looking in the other direction; he's not looking back. And that's why I've always felt more akin to Faulkner's Quentin Compson than to anybody else in his fiction because he's trying to get away from it. He is sick of time, because time means the past and history. So he tears the hands off the watch. He's wandering around this godforsaken Boston suburb, and the last place he wants to go is back to Mississippi, to time and history. . . . So I suppose, I would like to think of starting where Faulkner left off, of starting with a Quentin Compson who DIDN'T commit suicide. Suicide is easy. Keeping Quentin Compson alive is something else.[1]

Percy's declaration of independence from the Faulkner tradition is obviously over-simplified. His protagonists may be "looking forward," but they are looking backward as well, their minds shaped by the inescapable past. Still, his interest in Quentin Compson and in the theme of suicide is, I think, a defining point both for understanding his relationship to Faulkner and for gauging how Percy's fiction represents an advancement in the development of the Southern fictional hero, from suicidal despairer to creature of hope. Stated differently, the issue of suicide marks a distinction between the humanistic perspective of Faulkner and the religious vision of Percy. Other critics have already discussed the biographical and psychological importance of suicide in Percy's life and work. My aim is to explore the notion of spiritual suicide in terms of what it means for Percy to be a 20th century Southern writer. I will concentrate on two central and inter-related aspects of suicide: first, the problem of language; and secondly, the problem of sexuality. Both of these aspects of the theme of suicide are integral to Faulkner's and Percy's portrayal of the figure of the modern writer, whom Percy, including himself, calls an ex-suicide. Moreover, I will argue that much of Percy's fictional portrayal of the predicament of the modern writer is in direct response to the issues concerning suicide and the writer raised by Faulkner in his depiction of Quentin Compson.

I.

The theme of suicide undergoes significant transformation in Percy's fiction in comparison with Faulkner. Although the actuality or the threat of literal suicide is a recurrent theme in all of his novels, Percy—influenced by Kierkegaard—is more interested in the condition of spiritual suicide, the death-in-life of despair. Despair for Kierkegaard is the refusal to will to be a self, to be that union of the finite and the infinite which can find identity only "transparently under God."[2] The refusal to be a self entails a denial of the spirit, or "suicide." Kierkegaard also argues that to be in despair is "not to able to die"; it is to suffer a "sickness unto death." One can say, then, conversely, that self which is able to "die" or relinquish an inauthentic selfhood to become an authentic self "transparently under God" can be called an "ex-suicide."

All of Percy's novels reveal how much Kierkegaard's idea of despair as spiritual suicide dominates his vision, far beyond but not unrelated to the concern with literal suicide. Despair permeates every novel, exemplified by the self "refusing to be itself"—by role-playing, by bestialism, by deference to experts, by objectification, and by suicide itself. So pervasive is despair in his work that one can speak of a condition of cultural suicide or general thanatos; yet his protagonists also struggle against it, struggle, that is, to become ex-suicides.

Percy adds a semiotic dimension to Kierkegaard's idea of selfhood and suicide. What defines the self as uniquely human for Percy is the ability to use language. Selfhood means exercising the power to name reality. Semiotically, to be a self is to be a namer; conversely, semiotic "suicide" is silence before reality, what Kierkegaard termed "shut-up-ness." For Percy, naming is the triadic communion of a namer, something to be named, and an other with which to share the communication. Although Percy rarely elaborated the point, the existence of a First Namer, a divine source who empowers man to know and name reality, is implied clearly.

However, Percy also affirmed that the self cannot name itself definitively; it is "unformulable" because ". . . once the self locates itself at the dead center of its world, there is no signified to which a signifier can be joined to make a sign. The self has no sign of itself. No signifier applies. All signifiers apply equally."[3] Percy identifies this dilemma with the fall into self-consciousness. "From the moment the signifying self turned inward and became conscious of itself, trouble began as the sparks fly up. . . . The exile from Eden is, semiotically, the banishment of the self-conscious self from its own world of signs" (*Cosmos*, 107-108). This "catastrophe" is the semiotic version of Kierkegaard's existential situation of despair—the failure of the power to name truth. Yet the hope of redemption is alike in both models. In Kierkegaard, the creature struggles against despair to discover itself as spirit "transparently under God" and embrace the freedom to act. In the semiotic model, the creature can escape the solipsism of the unformulable self that attends the breakthrough into language by finding community with fellow creatures and con-celebrating reality in language under the power of a First Namer. For Percy "The self in a world is rich or poor accordingly as it succeeds in identifying its otherwise unspeakable self, e.g. mythically, by identifying itself with a world sign, such as a totem; religiously, but identifying itself as a creature of God" (*Cosmos*, 122). Language itself suffers devaluation when "the signified becomes encased in a simulacrum like a mummy in a mummy case," but the literary artist can redeem it: ". . . a recovery is possible. The signified can be recovered from the ossified signifier. . . . A poet can wrench signified out of context and exhibit it in all its queerness and splendor" (*Cosmos*, 105). The situation of the writer is both sign of the fall and exemplum of possible redemption.

Combining these semiotic and existential perspectives, it is possible to define an "ex-suicide" as one who affirms selfhood specifically under God as a namer. Conversely, a "suicide" refuses to become such a namer, choosing instead the despair of "shut-up-ness," or escaping the demands of authentic selfhood by deferring totally to the language and vision of another, which Kierkegaard calls being "defrauded by others." Finally, another form of semiotic despair is to affirm a self defiantly independent of any divine Power, wherein man alone is the measure of reality, a stance Kierkegaard termed "stoicism."

The second element I want to explore regarding the theme of suicide in Faulkner and Percy is sexuality. Percy did not say as much explicitly about this as he did about language, but his novels, especially *Lancelot*, show that sexuality is central to the concept of selfhood, and hence to "suicide" and "ex-suicide." As with language, sexuality is rooted in the mystery of human origins. It is not a question of gender *per se*, but of sexuality's ultimate derivation and meaning. Viewed from the perspective of myth, sexuality is seen as divine in origin, part of humanity's power to participate in transcendent creative mystery, analogous to the power of naming on the linguistic level. Following Kierkegaard, one can say that to become an authentic self is to become a unique sexual self "transparently under God," understanding sexuality as a mystery rooted in the paradox of humanity's finite/infinite nature. Any attempt to "solve" this mystery or to bifurcate sexuality into the dualism of divine/bestial (as Quentin Compson and Lance Lamar do) is necessarily reductive because it denies the paradox and mystery of sexuality.

Yet viewed from a purely historical or scientific perspective, sexuality is seen as definable solely by cultural and/or biological forces. The self as sexual agent is viewed as autonomous; that is, it acts without reference to any divine Power as the source of creation and ultimate meaning, or so it assumes. Sexuality viewed from this perspective is analagous to the notion of a dyadic exchange in language, that it, as a mechanical exchange between organisms within an environment. Such a perspective, however, amounts to a state of spiritual "suicide," because the human self—that mystery of finite/infinite—effectively is denied. For Percy, however, language is a triadic event, flawed but nevertheless capable of recovering the "suicided" self. So also, the recovery of the authentically human character of sexuality is a triadic event—the concelebration of creation with another, in recognition of the mystery of the other, under God. Finally, the view of sexuality—whether religious/transcendent or historicist—is central to the issue of the self as namer, as creator, hence to the vocation of the writer. What kind of writer or namer emerges—IF indeed one emerges at all—is rooted in the figure of the artist's vision of the triad of self, language, and sexuality.

II.

Lewis P. Simpson has shown brilliantly how Quentin Compson can be seen as Faulkner's figure of the 20th century artist.[4] Simpson traces the nexus of sexuality, creativity, and history that came to focus in Faulkner's attempt to understand his vocation as writer in the face of a collapse of the transcendent meaning of religion, community, and family. He argues persuasively that Faulkner's dramatization of the writer's situation is represented most forcefully in *The Sound and the Fury*, because Quentin embodies both the writer's consciousness of the loss of transcendent meaning and his resistance to the devaluing forces of historicism. Moreover, Quentin's relationship with his sister Caddy conjoins the writer's awareness of the historicity of both sexuality and consciousness, an awareness of ". . . how in the modern world, bereft of mythic and traditional order save as this appears in the trappings of nostalgia, the 'dark, harsh flowing of time' is channeled directly into the sensitive self instead of the family and the community" (94). Quentin tries to wrest permanent meaning from this situation by positing a code of stoical family honor, but he fails miserably; fails, that is, in the role of artist-as-savior who creates order. His failure eventuates in literal suicide; his spiritual suicide as artist figure eventuates in silence—the final "peace" of chosen death—after he discovers, as Simpson puts it, that he is "no dying god (artist as sacrificial redeemer) but a world historical neurotic and self-defeated historian . . ." (95). The Quentin of *The Sound and the Fury*, then, represents Faulkner's acute awareness of the predicament of the modern literary artist: dedicated by vocation to locate meaning in experience through language, yet conscious also, under the impact of historicism, of the transitoriness, indeed the vacuousness, of the very instrument of meaning— language itself.

Although Quentin's relationship with Caddy is central to his identity, his relationship with his father is the primary locus for his role as a figure of the literary artist. The elder Jason Compson embodies a fatalism familiar in post-bellum Southern fiction. Mr. Compson's fatalistic vision is at one with his rhetoric, and Quentin's failure to overcome the language tradition of his father is as much responsible for his spiritual suicide as an incipient artist figure as his plunge into the Charles River. Quentin drowns in his father's rhetoric long before his actual death, a fact signified by his increasing acquiescence to his father's language and vision as the section unfolds, to the point of almost complete final identification of father and son. Quentin fails to become Kierkegaard's self as "spirit transparently under God" both personally (i.e. sexually) and linguistically, and the rhetoric of stoicism he comes to share with his father is the mark of his defeat as man and as artist figure.

Recalling Kierkegaard's definition of stoicism as a form of defiant despair, I would describe Mr. Compson's language as a rhetoric of stoicism characterized by devaluation, reductiveness, and closure to mystery. His rhetoric excludes any meaningful point of reference to a transcendent spiritual order. Such a rhetoric also implies a devaluation and relativizing of language itself, since it denies implicitly any ultimate source of truth expressible in words. Stated differently, the collapse of values witnessed in Mr. Compson is coextensive with his sense of the collapse of language into meaninglessness, a situation Quentin as incipient artist figure must try to contend against.

We see the overpowering influence of Mr. Compson's stoical rhetoric in this tale ". . . full of sound and fury/Signifying nothing" from the opening page of the Quentin section, when he declares the "reducto absurdum of all human experience," that battles are neither fought nor won because "the field only reveals to man his own folly and despair, and victory is an illusion of philosophers and fools."[5] Quentin tries to counter his father's despairing vision with his own stoically abstract code of honor, but he is eventually overwhelmed by his father to the point of self-oblivion. He is, as Kierkegaard would say, "defrauded by another," his own father. Moreover, Quentin's deference to his father's language and vision is intimately bound up with his role as symbolic artist figure. His most decisive failure as "storyteller" in the novel is his failure to convince his father in their imaginary conversation that he has committed incest with Caddy. His father knows he is incapable of such an act, but more importantly, to Mr. Compson the words themselves do not even signify because the act has no ethical meaning. "It's nature is hurting you not Caddy and I said that's just words and he said So is virginity and I said you don't know. You can't know and he said Yes. On the instant when we come to recognize that tragedy is second-hand" (143).

Mr. Compson's stoical rhetoric also includes an explicit rejection of logocentric Christianity, the Divine Word incarnated in history, and this form of despair also marks Quentin indelibly. Speaking of his mother, Quentin says that "she couldn't see that Father was teaching us that all men are just accumulations dolls stuffed with sawdust swept up from the trash heaps where all previous dolls had been thrown away the sawdust flowing from what wound in what side that not for me died not" (218).

Quentin's failure to affirm an authentic self is denoted by his increasing acquiescence to his father's stoical rhetoric, especially to Mr. Compson's reductive historicist view of sexuality. This occurs in spite of Quentin's presumed defense of sexual honor regarding women. As he wanders the streets of Boston, Quentin thinks (and we note the identification of son and father here): "Father and I protect women from one another from themselves our women. . . ." But his inner paternal voice quickly responds:

> *Women are like that* they don't acquire knowledge of people we are for that they are just born with a practical fertility of suspicion that makes a crop every so often and usually right they have a natural affinity for evil for supplying whatever the evil lacks in itself for drawing it about them instinctively as you do bedclothes in slumber fertilizing the mind for it until the evil has served its purpose *whether it ever existed or no.* (119)

Later, Quentin fully assumes his father's view of female sexuality as evil by generalizing it into a cosmological image of the origins of sexuality:

> Because women so delicate so mysterious Father said.
> Delicate equilibrium of periodical filth between two
> moons balanced. Moons he said full and yellow as har-
> vest moons her hips thighs. Liquid putrefaction like
> drowned things floating. . . . (159)

Caught in a dualism that sees sexuality and women as either transcendent vessels of purity or as corruptly bestial, and therefore unhuman, Quentin tries to claim incest with Caddy. As many critics have observed, the claim of incest is a mask for Quentin's own narcissism and inability to love. In this sense, incest represents the ultimate destructive inversion of the self—Kierkegaard's state of sin—an act of egoistic closure and refusal "to die" to the other in love which is the psychospiritual equivalent of the despair of "shut-up-ness" on the linguistic level.

With the collapse of his "story" about incest and thus the collapse of his desparate attempt to claim an autonomous self as storyteller, Quentin moves inexorably toward literal suicide, echoing his father's despair. Significantly, their final colloquy concerns the bankruptcy of words and deeds, and the key term in the colloquy—"temporary"—sums up the historicist compulsion. When Mr. Compson insists that even Quentin's despair over Caddy will pass because everything is "temporary," Quentin thinks: "And then, I'll not be. *Non fui. Sum fui. Non sum.*" Quentin argues for suicide as a decisive act of manhood, but even this act is rendered meaningless by his father's cynicism. When Mr. Compson says "we must just stay awake and see evil done for a little while its not always," Quentin responds:

> . . . it doesn't even have to be that long for a man of
> courage and he do you consider that courage and i yes sir
> don't you and he every man is the arbiter of his own
> virtues whether or not you consider it courageous is of
> more importance than the act itself than any act other-
> wise you could not be in earnest and i you don't believe i
> am serious and he i think you are too serious to give me
> any cause of alarm you wouldn't have felt driven to the
> expedient of telling me you have committed incest
> other-wise and i i wasn't lying and he you wanted to
> sublimate a piece of natural human folly into a horror
> and then exorcise it with truth and i it was to isolate
> her out of the loud world so that it would be as though

it had never been and did you try to make her do it and
i i was afraid to i was afraid she might and then it
wouldn't have done any good but *if i could tell you we
did it it would have been so* and then the others
wouldn't be so and then the world would roar away. . . .
(219-220) (My italics)

Mr. Compson discounts Quentin's threat of suicide, because "No
man ever does that under the first fury of despair or remorse or
bereavement he does it only when he has realized that even the
despair of remorse or bereavement is not particularly important
to the dark diceman . . ."; he says his son "will not do that until
you have come to believe that even she was not quite worth despair perhaps. . . ." Quentin denies that he will ever come to
such a view, but he fixes on the word "temporary," which signifies the irresistable relativity and final meaninglessness of all action and language: ". . . and i temporary it will be better for me
for all of us and he every man is the arbiter of his own virtues
but let no man prescribe for another mans well-being and i temporary and he was the saddest word of all there is nothing else in
the world . . ." (221-222). So Quentin succumbs, a victim of his
father's despairing vision of language, sexuality, and indeed all
existence—a would-be teller of tales drowned into silence after a
life-long extinguishment of the self.

III.

    Percy's interest in a "Quentin Compson who didn't com-
mit suicide" and his interest in "keeping Quentin Compson
alive" was central to his self-definition as a Southern writer.
This self-definition meant coming to terms with suicide in the
Kierkegaardian sense; that is, as the relation between suicide understood as a refusal of "the self as spirit under God" and the vocation of writing itself. It meant subsuming yet passing beyond
Faulkner's figuration of the artist in Quentin to create a figure of
the artist as "ex-suicide." It meant moving beyond, both in vision and rhetoric, the closure of stoicism and the limits of
Faulknerian humanism into the mystery of the religious mode.
It meant coming to terms specifically with the two primary elements in Quentin's suicidal despair—language and sexuality.
    Percy's first three novels contain intimations of actual
suicide, seen in Kate Cutrer, Dr. Sutter and Dr. Tom More. Also,
the general cultural atmosphere in all three novels reveals that

renunciation of the self as spirit Kierkegaard defined as suicidal despair. Sexuality is also important in these three novels, but except in Dr. Sutter's journal, it is generally treated in a glancing, somewhat satirical manner. The issue of language—hence the writer's disposition toward language—is present also in these three novels, but as a recessive theme. Only with *Lancelot* did Percy begin to explore the meaning of spiritual suicide in direct relation to the meaning of sexuality and language. *Lancelot* seems to me the most crucial novel in Percy's canon, a turning point in his dramatic working out of his vocation as a Southern writer. Lancelot's situation most clearly resembles that of Quentin Compson as figure of the artist in *The Sound and the Fury*. The problem of spiritual suicide and the writer is not settled in *Lancelot*, but the novel is a crucial juncture from which Percy was then able to resolve "the matter of Quentin" in *The Second Coming*. In that novel, the suicide issue is resolved through Will Barrett's declaration of philosophical and linguistic freedom from his stoic father, his assumption of the symbolic artist's role as namer of the despair that haunts the age (like Percy), and perhaps most importantly, through the successful conjunction of sexuality and language in the creation of a new "language of love" between Will and Allison Huger.

Parallels between Quentin Compson and Lance Lamar are apparent even from a cursory glance, notwithstanding important differences. Lance's statement that the past is "feckless" echoes *in extremis* Percy's claim of unconcern with story-telling the past in order to come to terms with it; nevertheless, like Quentin's, Lance's monologue is obsessed with the past. Still, Percy's claim suggests that on one level the novel is *about* the uselessness of trying to come to terms with the past through autonomous self-scrutiny by either protagonist or writer. This amounts to a critique from a religious viewpoint of Faulkner's general practice, because the only way from a religious point of view to "escape" the past and live freely in the present is through repentence, forgiveness, and conversion to a new life achieved by admission of one's "noughtness" under God. For Percy, to be obsessed as Lance is with scrutinizing and recreating the past autonomously is to invite solipsism and despair. In this sense Lance's monologue can be seen as Percy the religious writer's exorcism of those dark impulses toward the rhetoric of stoicism and humanism always latent in his vision. Percy saw a demonic element in writing (as well as sexual and theological

ones); hence Lance can be seen as a projection of the artist as de-
mon, a self possessed, as Kierkegaard would say, by a demonic
voice revealed in Lance's savage indictment of the age and in his
blindness to his own flaws.[6] Rhetoric for Lance becomes in part
an elaborate "false show" that masks his inner being from himself.

Quentin and Lance are mirrored in several other ways as
well. Both are half-mad narrators, sons of weak fathers. Both
are obsessed with the collapse of values, specified by sexual betrayal within the family; both are obsessed with retrieving lost
honor. Both are involved in symbolically incestuous relationships with female family members. Both agonize over the failure of love, and more deeply, over the devaluation of sexuality
in history. Both are governed by dualistic, reductive views of
women. Both face crises over the meaning and value of action,
choosing obverse forms of violence—suicide and murder—in
response to their situations. Both are tale-tellers who try unsuc-
cessfully to convince father-figure listeners, but while Quentin
finally identifies with his father, Lance is unable either to convert Fr. John to his neo-stoicism or to accept the Christian view
implied in the priest-confessor's role, a key difference between
the two novels. Both novels deal centrally with the problem of
language as a key to defining the self, especially the sexual-
linguistic self as spirit. In sum, Lance can be seen as a symbolic
figure of the writer through whom Percy explored the meaning
of his own vocation in relation to the Southern tradition, much
as Faulkner did through Quentin. Lance is Percy's version of the
modern writer's struggle over what Lewis P. Simpson has called
the historicism of mind, the solipsistic condition.

Study of the two conjoined elements of language and sexuality reveal deeper implications of the parallel between
Quentin and Lance. Quentin is unable to make Caddy's acts of
sexual lust commensurate with the concepts of honor, virginity,
and love he tries to uphold. He cannot make the act commensurate with the word. Lance Lamar also explores the conjoined
meaning of sexuality and language. Lance argues that the sex act
is "incommensurate" with any other experience, absolutely
unique, and therefore incapable of definition. It is "unspeakable," he implies, because it involves the mystery of personality;
it is an "ecstasy" (ex-stasis, i.e. literally "out of place"), wherein
the self may "lose" itself yet also "find itself" in the other. Because the self as spirit is finite/infinite, the mystery of the sex act

involves both divine and demonic potentialities, which Lance notes when he overhears Margot and her lover cry out "—God" and "—shit" during their ecstatic love-making. But though he affirms the "unformulable" mystery of the sex act, affirms its "unspeakable" nature, in the end Lance embraces Mr. Compson's historicist view of sex and women just as fatally as Quentin did. Like Quentin, to Lance women become either idealized ladies or whores, never real mysterious persons, a truth revealed when he claims to have found the "great secret of life"—that men and women are born to violate and be violated by each other. His view represents a totally reductive collapse of the transcendent religious or mythical views of sexuality, into the bestialism of a purely mechanistic view of sex in history. Unlike Quentin, Lance seems to overcome the impotence of his situation by his sexual assault on the actress Raine. But Lance's act of bestial possession only fulfills the demonic potentiality of sexuality; though he claims to "know" her through sex, his assault is a perversion of the mystery of human communion in the sexual act, a mystery that literally escapes him.

Still, Lance also rages against this collapse of the value and meaning of sexuality, even as he tries to affirm its mystery by his pseudo-religious, blasphemous references to Margot's sex, as the "ark of the covenant" where he eats "communion." So also, as a figure of the artist, he attempts to destroy mystery with language even as he affirms the incommesurability of experience with language. In his despair, he presumes to attempt to "define" evil by his search for the meaning of sin, just as he tries to define the ontology of sexuality. In this role as autonomous Knower and Sayer, he would supplant God, recognizing no dependence on a divine source of naming. But in this attempt to know all in order to say all, he becomes the demonic rationalist as artist. His vision and rhetoric, like Mr. Compson's, bear all the marks of the closure and reductiveness of stoicism. Lance as namer is Percy's dramatization of the "logically" insane end of the rationalist who defiantly chooses autonomy rather than become the "ex-suicide" namer as "nought" under God. Fittingly, Lance is linked with Satan at the end of the novel, the demonic destroyer of truth and mystery whom Fr. Smith in *The Thanatos Syndrome* calls the great "depriver of meaning."

Like Quentin, Lance would also assume the role of artist as savior, seen in his plan to revive the lost code of honor and female virtue in his new colony in Virginia. But Lance's utopia, based on sexual dualism and gnostic pride, is as unworldly and unrealistic as Quentin's desire for a private world for himself and Caddy. Anna knows this and so rejects Lance's plan. And again like Quentin, Lance is driven by the illusory figures of the idealized feminine and the stoical father. Lance's duplicitous mother Lily guides him to revenge and to "overcome" the impotence of his father, thereby ironically fulfilling Mr. Compson's pronouncement to Quentin that "no Southern gentleman ever disappoints a lady. . . ."

As a projected artist figure, Lance may well represent a kind of exorcism for Percy the satirist. Lance's reductive view of experience is co-extensive with his reductive deployment of language in the savage and univocal condemnation of the age. Hence Lance's monologue can be seen as Percy's self-reflexive critique of the dark side of his own satiric impulses, a critique necessary in order to achieve balance. That balance is achieved in the "silent" voice of Fr. John in the novel, the crucial religious voice that distinguishes Lance's situation from that of Quentin. Quentin drowns in his father's stoicism, but Lance has available a "fatherly" voice and vision that avoids closure, one that constantly resists Lance's stoic code and prods him toward deeper self-understanding. Fr. John constantly asks Lance about love—did he love Margot?—trying to lead him to an awareness of the mystery of human relationships. About God he is largely silent, but his silence works effectively to undermine the narrative Lance develops in order to justify himself as actor and storyteller. Whether Lance is lying or not becomes secondary to the *intent* of his story-telling. In the end, Lance is damned out of his own mouth, his rage a mark of his suicidal despair. But his presence and the few words spoken by Fr. John offer the hope of an alternative vision of reality, one signified by the open form of the novel's ending.

Still, this possibility of a way out of the closure of stoicism—i.e. the possibility of the religious—is presented obliquely in *Lancelot*. So also, the possibility of a way out of spiritual suicide, focussed on language and sexuality, is presented marginally through Anna, who rarely speaks except to denounce Lance's dualism. Only in *The Second Coming* did Percy fully explore the triadic relationship of language, sexuality, and the self as "spirit transparently under God." In that exploration he transformed "the matter of Quentin"—the figure of the artist as hero—by moving beyond Faulkner and the ethos of stoicism and humanism into the fully dramatized religious mode. Will Barrett is Percy's most fully developed figure of the writer as an "ex-suicide," the prophet as "nought" who explores the religious meaning of man's predicament in the 20th century. Barrett triumphs over both the threat of actual suicide and over the condition of spiritual suicide which permeates his life, the legacy of his stoical father. And the triumphs are focussed specifically in those defining elements of selfhood—sexuality and language—conjoined in Barrett's loving relationship with Allison Huger.

Parallels to Quentin's situation again abound in *The Second Coming*, but Percy's move beyond *Lancelot* is decisive. Like Quentin, Barrett struggles against his father's deadly stoicism, but he is much more self-conscious of his predicament than either Quentin or Lancelot. Barrett knows that he and his father are not "pals." In Will's reference to him as "old mole," he recognizes their reenactment of the struggle between the half-"mad" son who anguished over the emptiness of language, the "fall" of female sexuality and suicide, and the all-demanding dead father—that is, Hamlet himself. Yet unlike Quentin, Will knows that although his father literally missed killing him on their hunting trip, he infected him with a despair that governed most of his life. "By now I have learned something and been surprised by it after all. Learned what? That he didn't miss me after all, that I thought I survived and I did but I've been dead of something ever since and didn't know it until now." Will discovers that he is a spiritual suicide.

Again, as in Quentin's case, the father's suicidal vision is linked to a mechanistic view of sexuality. Eros alone, untransformed by love, becomes thanatos. Will sees this when he recalls his father's attempt to murder him.

> . . . I cleaned the gun when I got it back from the sheriff in Mississippi. Both barrels. Wouldn't one have been enough? Yes, given an ordinary need for death. But not if it's a love of death. In the case of love, more is better than less, two twice as good as one, and most is best of all. And if the aim is the ecstasy of love, two is closer to infinity than one, especially when the two are twelve gauge Super-X number eight shot. And what samurai self-love of death, let alone the little death of everyday fuck-you, can match the double Winchester come of taking yourself into yourself, the cold steel extension of oneself into mouth, yes, for you, for me, for us, the logical and ultimate act of fuck you love fuck-off

> world, the penetration and perfect union of perfect cold
> gunmetal with warm quailing mortal flesh, the coming
> to end all coming. . . .[7]

As suicide is equated with an ultimate, solipsistic sexual orgasm,
so also is living in the fallen world equated with sexual and spiritual impotence.   The parallel to Quentin is clear—impotence
and incestuous self-absorption culminating in suicide, the only
alternative to despair.

> "*You're one of us*, his father said.
> Yes, very well. I'm one of you. You win.
> Where does such rage come from? From the discovery
> that in the end the world yields only to violence, that
> only the violent bear it away, that short of violence all
> is in the end impotence?" (171)

Lance Lamar chooses violence in his attempt to overcome spiritual and sexual impotence, but Will Barrett does not. Unlike
Quentin and Lance, Will finds a locus of meaning and an
authentic self by finding the secret to overcome suicide. The
secret is both his love with Allison Huger, which transforms
eros into caritas through a new language, and the gift he receives
to *name*, and break free of, the destructive influence of his
father's stoic rhetoric. Will names death in all its forms,
becoming the figure of the artist as ex-suicide namer who gains
power over creation by his acts and words. Will's conversion
occurs after his thwarted attempt at suicide in the cave, comes in
the form of God's oblique "answer" to his quest and in the gift of
Allison.

Percy's transformation of the dilemma of sexuality and
language raised in Quentin Compson and in Lance is achieved
in the relationship between Will and Allison, where the dual
mysteries of language and sexual love are linked. Listening to
Will speak, Allie finds that

> She could not hear the words for listening to the way
> he said them. Was he saying the words for the words
> themselves, for what they meant, or for what they
> could do to her? . . . Though he hardly touched her, his
> words seemed to flow across all parts of her body. Were
> they meant to? A pleasure she had never known before
> bloomed deep in her body. Was this a way of making
> love? (262)

In their love-making, Allie and Will's verbal communication is
as integral to the act as their physical union. Allie's previous af-
fair with Sarge was simply a physical exchange, literally selfless

and therefore filled with despair. But with Will it is different. They discover a fresh language of love, not the deathly rhetoric of convention; they "make it new" and "sing a new song," something Percy insisted the writer must do to overcome the dead weight of convention and tradition. As they unite, Allie links the linguistic and the sexual in their feelings.

> The good is all over me, starting with my back. Now I understand how the two work.
> What two?
> The it and the doing, the noun and the verb, sweet sweet love and a putting it to you, loving and hating, you and I." (263)

The union of the "it and the doing, the noun and the verb," in the mystery of love enacts the triadic mystery of language which for Percy is the defining element of the human self as spirit. "A particularly mysterious property (of language) is the relation between the sign (signifier) and the referent (signified). It is expressed by the troublesome copula 'is,' when Helen (Keller) said that the perceived liquid 'is' water (the word). It 'is' but then again it is not" (*Cosmos*, 96). Allie's realization of this mystery of language—the mystery of the "troublesome copula" seen now as their union—transforms her experience of sex into the mystery of love, as it does equally for Will. The unhuman dualism of Quentin and Lance is left behind.

But in his break with his father Will most clearly assumes the figurative role of artist, the namer as ex-suicide. Threatening suicide when he descents into the cave, Will challenges God to prove His existence. His quest is an inversion of Lance's demonic quest for the meaning of sin, its passive form reminescent of Quentin's suicide by drowning. Although Will receives no direct answer to his hubristic quest/question, the signs that he does receive are enough to convert him from suicide to ex-suicide. Saved by a toothache and cared for lovingly by Allie, he returns to become the namer who triumphs over the stoic vision of his father by affirming his selfhood against the forces of death. For the "secret" he discovers, the revelation given him, is one that Quentin and Lance failed to find—the knowledge of this century's, his father's, and his own love of death. But now he can stand over against it and name it.

> Ha, there is a secret after all, he said. But to know the secret answer, you must first know the secret question.
> The question is, who is the enemy?

> Not to know the enemy is already to have been killed by him. *Ha*, he said . . . *I do know. I know. I know the name of the enemy.*
> The name of the enemy is death. Not the death of dying but the living death. The name of this Century is the Century of the Love of Death." (272)

After naming a long category of the forms of death in this century, Will claims his own life by rejecting his father, who is now equated with the "old Father of lies . . . ," Satan himself. Analogously, Will as artist figure becomes the "nought" who finds his authentic voice and self "transparently under God." Percy moves beyond Faulkner to affirm the religious connection between earthly namer and the ultimate Source of word and vision. "You gave in to death, old mole, but I will not have it so. It is a matter of knowing and choosing. To know the many names of death is also to know there is life. I choose life. . . ." To knowing and choosing must also be added the central fact of the prophetic writer as ex-suicide—naming.

> Death in the form of death genes shall not prevail over me, for death genes are one thing but it is something else to name the death genes and know them and stand over against them and dare them. I am different from my death genes and therefore not subject to them. My father had the same death genes but he feared them and did not name them and thought he could roar out old Route 66 and stay ahead of them or grab me and be pals or play Brahms and keep them, the death genes, happy, so he fell prey to them.
> Death in none of these guises shall prevail over me, because I know all the names of death. (274)

Unlike Quentin's colloquy with his father, or the unreconciled colloquy between Lancelot and Fr. John, Will's colloquy with his father end in his total rejection of the elder Barrett's stoicism. But in separating himself from his earthly father Will implicitly finds intimations of another. In an apocalyptic vision following his litany against death, Will intuits the presence of an Other—a gift-giver—as the source of his knowledge and power to name.

> When he came to years from now, he was laying on the spot. No one was there. Yet something moved and someone spoke. Maybe it was D'lo. No. Was it Allie? No, nobody. No, somebody was there all right. Someone spoke: Very well, since you insisted on it, here it is, the green-stick, Rosebud, goldbug matador, the great distinguished thing.

> The ocean was not far away.
> As he turned to see who said it and who it was, there
> was a flash of light then darkness light again. (277)

The revelation, with its allusion to all the paths of suicidal despair ("Citizen Kane's" Rosebud; Poe's goldbug; Hemingway's matador and his suicide; the ocean at the end of Will's father's Route 66 escape trip, etc.), is the "answer" Will received to his demand for a sign from God. The revelation is mysterious yet clear, enabling him to name and renounce the "Father of lies," to love and act freely in the world, not crippled by his past or by stoicism. It also marks Percy's clearest declaration of his difference from Faulkner on the matter of Quentin as artist figure and as Southern writer himself. Percy moved beyond humanism, sensing its inadequacy as a response to the spiritual suicide of the age of despair. Through Will Barrett as figure of the artist as ex-suicide, he affirmed the sign of an ultimate Namer and Giver, made flesh in the Word and in the world of human love. Loving Allie, Will asks: "Is she a gift and therefore a sign of a giver? Could it be that the Lord is here, masquerading behind this simple silly holy face? Am I crazy to want both, her and Him? No, not want, must have. And will have" (360).

Percy's answer is yes, yes.

Notes

[1] Lawson, Lewis A. and Victor A. Kramer. *Conversations with Walker Percy.* Jackson: University of Mississippi Press, 1985, pp. 299-300. All further references cited in the text.

[2] Kierkegaard, Søren. *Fear and Trembling* and *The Sickness Unto Death.* Garden City, NY: Doubleday & Company, 1941, pp. 147-166 passim. All further references cited in the text.

[3] Percy, Walker. *Lost in the Cosmos.* New York: Farrar, Straus and Giroux, 1983, pp. 107-108. All further references cited in the text.

[4] Simpson, Lewis P. "Faulkner and the Legend of the Artist," in *Fifty Years After THE MARBLE FAUN,* George Core, ed. University, AL: University of Alabama Press, 1980, pp. 72-86 passim. All further references cited in the text.

[5] Faulkner, William. *The Sound and the Fury.* New York: Modern Library, 1929, p. 93. All further references cited in the text.

[6] See Percy's important Self-Interview, "Questions They Never Asked Me," in *Signposts in a Strange Land,* Patrick Samway, ed. New York: Farrar, Straus and Giroux, 1991, pp. 397-423.

⁷ Percy, Walker. *The Second Coming*. New York: Farrar, Straus and Giroux, 1980, pp. 148-149.

Love, Sex, and Knowledge in Walker Percy's *Lancelot*:
A Metaphysical View

Critics of Walker Percy's novel *Lancelot* have by now aptly shown that Lancelot Lamar's vision of women, sex, and evil is perversely distorted.[1] Yet while dramatizing this distortion, Percy also uses Lance's viewpoint to expose certain obsessions of the age, with Lance himself as the prime example. Lance's quest for the Unholy Grail—his search for the meaning of evil—is an abysmal failure, but as such it is the failure of all the simplistic moralists in our culture. Lance attempts to discover the meaning of sin and evil by investigating the meaning of human sexuality, specifically by uncovering his wife Margot's infidelity. He pursues this investigation both concretely and on a very high philosophical level, so that it becomes an exploration of some of the deepest mysteries of metaphysics and epistemology. Although Lance fails miserably in his quest, Percy the novelist does not, for through Lance he presents a profound analysis of the roots of sexual malaise in the 20th century.

Lance's quest for the meaning of sin and evil as manifested in human sexuality must be viewed in the broadest sense from a metaphysical perspective. Lance "discovers" his own life, he tells the listener Percival, when he ponders the question: "Can good come from evil? Have you ever considered the possibility that one might undertake a search not for God but for evil?"[2] These questions lead him to wonder if in fact there is such a thing as sin, and if so, whether it is demonstrable. "But what if you could show me a *sin*? a purely evil deed, an intolerable deed for which there is no explanation. Now there's a mystery . . . when was the last time you saw a *sin*?" (54). The question is deliberately taunting, as Percy intended, and Lance's search for an answer to it reveals Percy's complex strategy. Percy uses the question to probe a central truth about modern Western society—the loss of the sense of sin as a spiritual, metaphysical

reality, or to state the matter differently, the loss of a sense of sin
as a fundamental flaw in the order of being. Modern culture, as
Lance recognizes, has tried to reduce evil to an empirical datum.
In this culture human action is viewed as a naturalistic response
to needs, wants, and desires. Therefore an "evil act" is seen as
only a manifestation of behavioristic impulses.

> 'Evil' is surely the clue to this age, the only quest ap-
> propriate to the age. For everything and everyone's
> either wonderful or sick and nothing is evil.
> . . . .
> The mark of the age is that terrible things happen but
> there is no 'evil' involved. People are either crazy,
> miserable, or wonderful, so where does 'evil' come in?
> (145-146)

If looked at from the viewpoint of modern culture, an "evil act"
ought to be able to be understood as an item in a category of
needs, wants, and desires. But it is this categorization against
which Lance instinctively rebels, and rightly so, for he senses
that such a behavioristic view is inadequate to explain the mystery of evil. And yet at the same time he is personally drawn to
try to unravel the mystery.[3]

The starting point for Lance's metaphysical quest into the
meaning of evil is an investigation of the act of sex. By uncovering the meaning of sex he hopes to uncover the mystery of evil.
The fact that he identifies sex with love is the major blind spot
in his vision, a blindness that leads him to follow the same empirical principles he persistently condemns. Nevertheless, Lance
is right in his choice of a starting place to explore the mystery, because love is the central human activity; it is most definitive of
our nature as creatures. And about the sex act Lance poses the
decisive question: is it a purely biological act fulfilling human
needs, or is it of an entirely different order altogether, i.e. a
metaphysical act? Considering Margot's adultery, Lance says:

> Beyond any doubt she was beside herself and pos-
> sessed by something, someone? else. Such considera-
> tions have led me to the conclusion that, contrary to the
> usual opinion, sex is not a category at all. It is not
> merely an item on a list of human needs like food, shel-
> ter, air, but is rather an unique ecstasy, *ek-stasis*,
> which is a kind of possession. Just as possession by
> Satan is not a category. You smile. You disagree? Are
> you then one of the new breed who believe that Satan is
> only a category, the category of evil? (21)

Percy's language here is very precise and demands careful analysis. To be able to categorize an action means to be able to generalize about it, to name it and know it as one of a group. It is a way of understanding the act and being able to speak about it. Conversely, if the act is seen as unique, which Lance says the act of sex is, then it is outside of empirical categories of definition (*ek-stasis* = "out of place"). It cannot be known or "spoken of" in this way, and is therefore *unspeakable* in the literal sense of the term. In short, it is a metaphysical act, rooted in the mystery of individual human personality, whose absolute spiritual uniqueness in the order of being cannot be objectively categorized.

Although the conclusions Lance finally draws from his quest are false and destructive, his initial insistence on the metaphysical uniqueness of the sex act is accurate. What Lance intuits is the fundamental paradox in the sexual relationship, a mystery that is at the same time the source of his epistemological anguish. This paradox can be stated as follows: on the one hand, the sex act is potentially the most intimate act between a man and a woman, a communion in which they can come closest to knowing each other. Such a communion is both physical and spiritual, a communication of one's very being, and a way of knowing the other. Hence it is potentially most divine, an analogue of the Godhead's communion of love to man, the communion of Himself by which He is made known. Yet the sex acts also contains great potential for intimate betrayal—betrayal and desecration of the other human being *and* of the divine, the spiritual reality incarnated in the act. Lance acknowledges these opposing potentialities when he overhears Margot and Jacoby uttering "God. Sh—. God. Sh—." during their copulation.

> Why does love require the absolute polarities of divinity—obscenity? I was right about love: it is an absolute and therefore beyond all categories. Who else but God arranged that love should pitch its tent in the place of excrement? Why not then curse and call on God in an act of love? (257-258)

But the other part of the mystery of the sex acts stems from the fact that human beings are also absolutely unique. Because this is so, it is impossible to fully know the other in the act of sex, or to be known. Human nature is essentially unknowable by another human being; consequently it is impossible either to fully possess or be possessed by another human being. In this respect every human person is inviolable, a truth which the rape victim Anna states in her rejection of Lance. "'Are you suggesting,' she said to me, 'that I, myself, me, my person, can be violated by a *man*? You goddam men'" (272). To be inviolable is to possess an essential sacredness in the order of being; that is, as a metaphysical entity. This inviolable self can be partly communicated through love, and thus partly known. But it cannot be known by rape, nor simply by the physical act of sexual intercourse. However, Lance thinks the other can be known and possessed in this way. He claims to "know" the actress Raine when he seduces her, even invoking the Old Testament sense of the term:

> For what comes of being adult was this probing her for her secret, the secret which I had to find out and she wanted me to find out. The Jews called it knowing and now I know why. Every time I went deeper I knew her better. Soon I would know her secret. We were watching each other. We were going to know each other but one of us would know first and therefore win. I was coming closer, closer. We watched each other watching. It was a contest. She lost. (254-255)

But Lance is completely wrong. He no more "knows" Raine than the rapists who assaulted Anna knew her. The sex act remains a mystery that is essentially unspeakable; it is not a category of knowledge to be comprehended in this way.

Lance's epistemological anguish stems from the fact that he cannot accept this mystery of existence; he cannot tolerate not knowing. Thus his frustration is with the very essence of human existence and its limitations. Instead of accepting these limitations, he becomes an Ethan Brand and Roger Chillingsworth in modern dress, consumed by a demonic passion to plumb the heart of the mysteries of evil and sexuality. But to attempt to penetrate these mysteries intellectually is to exceed human limits, and this results in a perversion of the human and the sexual. Consequently, as Lance admits, he discovered "nothing" at the heart of the mystery. When he murders Jacoby, he "feels" only the interaction of molecules as the knife severs Jacoby's windpipe. Because of his flawed vision, he can only conclude that the "meaning" of life is sexual aggression between human beings.

This reductive quality of Lance's mind—the way it tries to collapse metaphysical mysteries into empirical categories—can also be seen in the spurious "logic" of his argument about sex as the supreme locus of good and evil.

> Could it be possible that since the greatest good is to be
> found in love, so is the greatest evil? Evil, sin, if it ex-
> ists, must be incommensurate with anything else.
> Didn't one of your saints say that the entire universe in
> all its goodness is not worth the cost of a single sin? Sin
> is incommensurate, right? There is only one kind of be-
> havior which is incommensurate with anything what-
> ever, in both its infinite good and its infinite evil. That
> is sexual behavior. The orgasm is the only earthly in-
> finity. Therefore it is either an infinite good or an infi-
> nite evil. (146-147)

Lance's initial supposition that "the greatest good is to be found
in love" is flawed on at least two grounds. First, he excludes divine love, and so fails to distinguish between kinds of love and
degrees of goodness in love. Because he has excluded God, who
is absolute love, Lance elevates human love to the level of an
absolute and thereby commits himself to a deformed idea of the
order of reality itself. Secondly, Lance mechanistically identifies
"love" with sexual gratification, the orgasm as "earthly infinity."

However, when it comes to the question of evil, Lance's
claim that sin is incommensurate with anything else is correct to
the extent that it identifies sin as a spiritual reality, as a flaw in
the order of being. As in the case of his analysis of sexuality,
Lance intuits that evil is a metaphysical mystery, not something
that can be subjected to empirical categorization. But no sooner
does he affirm this than Lance falls into the trap of reductive ab-
solutizing in claiming that "there is only one kind of behavior
which is incommensurate with anything whatever, in both its
infinite good and its infinite evil. That is sexual behavior. The
orgasm is the only earthly infinity." But in fact sexual behavior
is finite, and so Lance is mistaken both in his claim that it is incommensurate with "anything whatever" and in his all-or-
nothing conclusion that sex is "either an infinite good or an infinite evil." What his argument reveals is the Manichean tendency to separate good from evil, an ignorance of the metaphysical truth that evil is not a separate essence but can only exist as a
subject of good, as a condition which is part of an existing good.

Lance's intellectual confusion and contradictory arguments are of course crucial to understanding his own perverse
behavior in the novel. But equally important is the way in
which his collapse of metaphysics into reductive empirical categories reveals the loss of a sacramental view of reality in the age.
A sacrament represents the interpenetration of the divine and

the physical world, so that the physical becomes mysteriously an instrument or medium of grace. To "know" reality in a sacramental way is to acknowledge the divine spirit which is both manifested within and yet also mysteriously "beyond" the object world. To know reality in a sacramental way requires anagogical vision. Conversely, to betray this vision is to commit idolatry in a literal sense, by making the physical object itself absolutely equatable with the divine. Such a betrayal is evident in Lance's profane elevation of Margot's body to the level of a sacrament.

> . . . She stood naked before the mirror, hands in her hair, one knee bent, pelvis aslant. She turned to me and put her hands under my coat and in her funny way took hold of a big pinch of my flank on each side. Gollee. Could any woman have been as lovely? She was like a feast. I wanted to eat her. I ate her.
>
> That was my communion, Father—no offense intended, that sweet dark sanctuary guarded by the heavy gold columns of her thighs, the ark of her covenant. (182)

This false "divinizing" of the physical represents one Manichean extreme in Lance's thinking. The other is its opposite: Lance's view of sex and the physical as evil—as "shit." For him it must be either/or; he cannot tolerate the ambiguity and mystery inherent in a truly sacramental view of reality. Thus he rails against the qualified view of sexual behavior implicit in Percival's Catholicism, because it demands consideration of the uniqueness of the act and rejects simplistic categorization.

> Damn you and your God. Between the two of you, you should have got it straight and had it one way or the other. Either it's good or it's bad, but which ever way it is, goddam it say so. Only you don't. You fuck off somewhere in between. You want to have it both ways: good—but—bad only if—and so forth.
> . . . .
> I won't have it you way with your God-bless-every-thing-because-it's-good-only-don't-but-if-you-do-it's-not-so-bad. (187-188)

The sharp differences between Percival's and Lance's visions is a paradigm for the alternative metaphysical views of reality Percy sees available to the age. Percival's vision is based upon a metaphysics that neither rejects the physical nor elevates it arbitrarily to the level of the spiritual. It is a vision which sees matter and spirit conjoined, sees the world as fallen yet not totally depraved, and sees real being as dynamic and capable of transformation by grace. Appropriately, Percy emphasizes that Percival's new role as parish priest will be *dispensing the sacraments* to suburban housewives and Buick dealers. Lancelot, however, rejects this sacramental vision, and like America itself, he is doomed to try to reinvent the world along utopian lines. Lacking a proper metaphysic, he must also try to reinvent man, making him into an abstract model of either pure honor or depravity. But such a model is a fiction, and the worst aspect of it is that it denies the way man is truly constituted as a being—as a metaphysical mystery, fallen yet inviolable in his sacredness.

Notes

[1] See especially Lewis A. Lawson's "The Gnostic Vision in *Lancelot*," *Renascence* 32 (1979): 52-64; and Jac Tharpe's *Walker Percy*, Boston: G. K. Hall and Company, 1983, pp. 88-105.

[2] Walker Percy. *Lancelot*. New York: Avon Books, 1977, p. 53. All further references are to this edition and are cited in the text.

[3] Percy's narrative strategy involves a subtle blend of entrapment, sympathy, and revulsion. We readers are expected to sympathize with Lance's rejection of the reductive empirical viewpoint; and we acknowledge the heroic seriousness of his concerns. At the same time, we are led to judge and reject the perverse consequences to which Lance pushes his quest.

Revisioning *The Fall*:
Walker Percy and *Lancelot*

> ". . . this incalculable fall before the
> image of what we are. . . ."
> *The Myth of Sisyphus*, Camus

In conversations and interviews Walker Percy frequently acknowledged the influence of Albert Camus on his thought and art. Specifically, when speaking of his novel *Lancelot* Percy cited the direct influence of Camus's *The Fall*: "I worked on *Lancelot* for three years, and I owe a debt to Camus. In his novel *The Fall*, one man talked to another man, and that's the way it goes in mine. It's an interesting form and a difficult one, something like a dramatic morality play."[1]

Percy's comment here acknowledges a similarity in narrative strategy between *The Fall* and *Lancelot*—the use of a first person confessional dramatic monologue. Like Camus, Percy employed this strategy to construct a subtle and densely-layered tale that attempts to entrap both the "listener" and the reader in a complex web of sympathy, partial complicity, and judgement of the narrators, Clamence and Lance Lamar.[2] Such a strategy also enabled Camus and Percy both to exploit and examine one of the major concerns they shared as writers—the inherent duplicity of language in general, and the widespread breakdown of language in the 20th century in particular. Yet beyond their technical similarities, the two novels resonate with such powerful thematic echoes that it seems unimaginable that Percy was not also profoundly engaged and inspired by the issues raised in *The Fall*. The philosophical argument advanced by Clamence in *The Fall*, I believe, would have posed a serious challenge to Percy's religious beliefs. *Lancelot* can be seen on one level as a response to this challenge. On another level, if we understand *The Fall*, as Rene Girard does, as a work of Camusian self-criticism, the novel would have mirrored for Percy some of the dangers inherent in his own role as prophetic author, as one deeply imperiled by the very exercise of judgement that his identity as author compelled.[3]

For all their differences in cultural background and immediate situation, Clamence and Lance show a remarkable similarity in personality and temperament. Percy certainly would have been attracted by Camus's use of his narrator to impugn the moral failings of modern society. By citing Lermontov's *A Hero of Our Time* in the epigraph to *The Fall*, Camus alerts us that this is "in fact a portrait . . . not of an individual . . . (but) the aggregate of the vices of our whole generation in their fullest expression."[4] The ethos of this modern Inferno is encapsulated by Clamence when he observes that future historians can sum up modern man in one sentence: "He fornicated and read the papers" (6). In Percy's novel the medium has changed from print to television, but Lance's judgement of his culture, though couched in more extreme language, is essentially the same.

> The Northerner is at heart a pornographer. He is an abstract mind with a genital attached. His soul is at Harvard . . . His body lives at Forty-second street. . . . The Southerner? The Southerner started out a skeptical Jeffersonian and became a crooked Christian. . . . Do you want a portrait of the New Southerner? He is Billy Graham on Sunday and Richard Nixon the rest of the week. He calls on Jesus and steals, he's in business, he's in politics. . . .
>
> California? The West? That's where the two intersect: Billy Graham, Richard Nixon, Las Vegas, drugs, pornography, and every abstract disincarnate idea ever hit upon by man roaming the wilderness looking for habitation.[5]

Yet neither Clamence nor Lance, for all their prescience as observers, have escaped contamination by the age. Both men suffer a devastating collapse of honor that stems from pride manifested in a deep conviction of their superiority. Yet their specific acts—Clamence's indifference to the suicide's cry, and Lance's discovery of his wife Margot's infidelity—are but the objective correlatives used by Camus and Percy to explore the murky abyss of egotism both protagonists inhabit. The question they face, *ex poste facto*, is not how to retain honor, since this is impossible in such a world, or even strictly speaking how to recover it. Rather, the question is how to recover the *semblance* of honor, so as to forestall the ever-present temptation to suicide. Clamence's strategy is to adopt the Janus mask of judge-penitent, to appear to include himself among the sinners of a faithless age, but only so as to escape the judgement of others and lord it over them. Lance's way to attempt recovery of honor is first to commit murderous revenge on the sinners, and then try to create a New Eden in Virginia based on a code of stoical honor, of which he will be the final arbiter, just as Clamence is the final judge in his world.

Central to the issue faced by Camus and Percy in their respective narrative is the problem of judgement. The role of judge assumed by Clamence and Lancelot is ultimately linked to the theological question of innocence and the origin of evil, and perforce to God's role in human history. Clamence believes that all humans are guilty and that redemption is unattainable. For him, Jesus is guilty because of the massacre of the Holy Innocents, which spared his own life; and his crucifixion, Clamence argues, merely confirmed Jesus's inability to live with such guilt. Clamence focuses on Jesus's cry of abandonment on the cross— "Why hast Thou forsaken me?"—though significantly he avoids mentioning Jesus's final acceptance of his sacrifice. Ultimately, of course, it is God Himself who Clamence holds responsible for the loss of innocence. The present condition of humanity, without belief in God or hope for redeeming grace, is for Clamence a condition in which judgement is separated from innocence, as signified by the stolen panel of the tryptich called "The Just Judges" which he possesses. Given this condition of universal guilt and judgement, Clamence's strategy is to proclaim his own infamy so as to win the right to judge others, and thereby claim an exalted position over them.

> ... I grow taller, I breathe freely, I am on the mountain, the plain stretches before my eyes. How intoxicating to feel like God the Father and to hand out definitive testamonials of bad character and habits. I sit enthroned among my bad angels at the summit of the Dutch heaven and I watch ascending toward me, as they issue from the fogs and the water, the multitude of the Last Judgement. They rise slowly; I already see the first of them arriving. On his bewildered face, half hidden by his hand, I read the melancholy of the common condition and the despair of not being able to escape it. And as for me, I pity without absolving, I understand without forgiving, and above all, I feel at last that I am being adored! (143)

Clamence's provisional ascendency is, however, also his isola-
tion, because in his fall into self-knowledge he discovered that
for him, love was simply another mask for egoistic manipulation and sensuality. "I conceived at least one great love in my
life, of which I was always the object," Clamence admits, and
then confesses to "a sort of congenital inability to see in love
anything but the physical" (59).

For Lance Lamar, the loss of innocence is linked to humanity's sexual nature as constituted by God at the creation.
Like Clamence, he finds God the culprit and arraigns Him before
the bar of judgement.

> The innocence of children. Didn't your God say that un-
> less you become as innocent as one of these, you shall not
> enter the kingdom of heaven?
>   Yes, but what does that mean?
> It is obvious he made a mistake or else played a very
> bad trick on us. Yes, I remember the innocence of child-
> hood. Very good! But then after awhile one makes a
> discovery. One discovers that there is a little secret
> God didn't let us in on. One discovers your Christ did
> not tell us about it. Yet God himself so arranged it that
> you wake up one fine morning with a thundering hard-
> on and wanting nothing more in life than a sweet hot
> cunt to put it in, drive some girl, any girl, into the
> ground, and where is the innocence of that? Is that part
> of the innocence? If so, he should have said so. From
> child to assailant through no doing of one's own—is
> that God's plan for us? Damn you and your God. (188)

From this Lance concludes that history is governed by a single
principle—that human beings are made either to commit or to
submit to sexual violation. His reduction of love to physical lust
echoes that of Clamence. Although he doesn't claim the self-
conscious and duplicitous role of judge-penitent as Camus's
hero does, Lance's own remorseless judgement of others reveals
in him the same attempt at personal exculpation and ascendency
that Clamence practices.

Yet if Percy's novel echoes many of the issues raised in
The Fall—innocence and universal guilt, God and history, egotism and self-vindication—Camus's particular emphasis on the
inescapability of judgment would have struck an especially res-
onant note with Percy for the two reasons I noted earlier. First, it
posed a challenge to his Christian beliefs. Secondly, it dramatized the predicament both writers shared as "prophetic" au-
thors. If both *The Fall* and *Lancelot* can be read as novels of self-

criticism, then for Percy, I believe, the challenges raised by Camus's novel pushed him in *Lancelot* to question and find a justification for both his own religious belief and his practice as a moralist writer. The strategic response he devised in the novel to the first challenge—to his religious belief—is integrally related to the answer he discovered for the second—the challenge to his position as moralist author.

In his brilliant essay "Camus's Stranger Retried," Rene Girard demonstrated how in *The Fall* Camus analyzed his own motives in writing *The Stranger* and discovered the roots of egoistic self-justification underlying his treatment of Meursault's fate. Camus's "case" against the judges in *The Stranger*, Girard argues, reveals the author's passionate ambition as a writer to place himself self-righteously on the side of the "innocent" martyr against the inhumane and indifferent system of judgement. The sympathy Camus affords Meursault, and creates for him in the reader, is balanced by the resentment the novel generates against the judges. Both qualities in *The Stranger* lead inexorably to the incredible conclusion that Meursault is condemned not for the murder which he committed, but because, as Camus stated in his preface to the novel: "A man who does not cry at the funeral of his mother is likely to be sentenced to death." The fundamental contradiction in the novel's argument, a contradiction summed up by the opposing terms "innocent" and "murder," only becomes fully apparent, Girard argues, in the light cast by *The Fall*. In the latter novel, Camus came to question his own motives as a writer who judges, who had judged and condemned the judges, and who now possessed sufficient knowledge of his own egoistic passion for self-justification to represent in Clamence the condition of authorial "bad faith" he had fallen into in writing *The Stranger*. Recognizing in Clamence's duplicitous role of judge-penitent his own duplicity in vindicating the accused *in order to* condemn the judges in *The Stranger*, Camus was able in *The Fall* to pose the deeper question of the pervasive evil of judgment itself. He saw that as an author he was not an "innocent" outsider like Meursault, that he too belonged to a community which engaged in unrelenting judgement and condemnation of fellow human beings. As Girard demonstrates, Camus had discovered who we are in the 20th century: "We are not healthy pagans. We are not Jews either, since we have no Law. But we are not real Christians, since we keep judging" (quoted in *Girard*, 34). There is one "law," of course, which speaks to this condition: the law of love expressed in St. Paul's epistles and implied in the admonition: "Thou art inexcusable, O Man, whosoever thou art that judgest; for wherein thou judgest another, thou condemnest thyself; for thou that judgest dost the same things." But in *The Fall*, the infernal condition of life without mercy is finally inescapable.

Like Camus, in *Lancelot* Percy questioned his own motives in writing within the narrative itself, especially his motives in judging the culture. However, unlike the young Camus who wrote *The Stranger*, Percy had few illusions about his intentions as an author who judges. Shortly after the publication of his first novel, *The Moviegoer*, he described in a letter to Caroline Gordon his "main problem as a fiction writer. . . . What I really want to do is tell people *what they must do and what they must believe if they want to live*."[6] This desire was a benign version of a corrolary impulse in Percy's sensibility: his deep passion to justify himself as a writer by judging (and often condemning) a society that refuses or fails to know how to live. That Percy was aware of the ambivalence of this deep passion is evident. In several interviews, and most importantly in his crafty yet revealing self-interview published in *Esquire*, Percy emphasized how malice and a demonic element—a passion to attack, judge and condemn—was a powerful motivating force behind all his fiction.[7] And in the same self-interview, he acknowledged an especially intimate and complex relationship between himself as writer and his protagonist Lance Lamar (422).

Throughout the novel Lance is an unrelenting moralist and judge, and to that extent he represents something of Percy's own ambitions as a writer and critic of culture, as well as his deep passion for self-justification. But Lance is a moralist taken to an insane, demonic extreme, and that qualification is most crucial. Judgement and condemnation become for Lance a means to escape from self-knowledge, a desire projected in his plan for a New Order of society in Virginia (similar to Clamence's new order, with himself as sole judge). Percy identifies *to a certain degree* with Lance's attacks on the moral pollution that surrounds him. (It is significant in this regard that much of Lance's animus is directed against the Hollywood movie industry, that familiar symbol of a morally bankrupt American culture, because insofar as stereotypical movie-making in *Lancelot* represents a corruption of art, it also constitutes a direct threat to his role as moralist-writer.) But for all his intimate connection with his protagonist, by creating Lance as a judge/moralist *in extremis* Percy distances himself from his narrator and employs him as a vehicle for self-examination and self-criticism of his motives as a writer, as Camus had done in *The Fall*.

One important clue to Percy's implicit self-criticism in *Lancelot*, I think, can be seen in the way the novel questions, inverts, and even undermines many themes and narrative patterns Percy so meticulously developed as serious statements of his beliefs in earlier novels and essays. (Percy's novels are always tantalizingly elliptical and oblique in depicting the persona of the writer, but *Lancelot* raises self-examination to an entirely different and more profound level. The humor of his earlier works is largely gone.) Percy puts into the mouth and actions of his half-mad narrator many of his most cherished concerns as a writer, and not just his usual targets of satirical attack. For example, the familiar Percyean theme of "coming to oneself" after some catastrophe, of awakening to self-awareness, is dramatized in Lance' s discovery of his wife Margot's adultery; but here the awakening leads to Lance's own adultery and sodomy, and his murderous revenge. Likewise, Percy's consuming preoccupation with language—with the possibility of intersubjective communion through language—as well as with the modern corruption of signs, is here cast in the form of Lance's attempt to communicate with the rape victim Anna who lives in the next cell. Lance hopes to convert her into the New Woman for his New Eden in Virginia, a hope which is at least partly dashed when Anna condemns Lance's paternalism. Like his creator, Lance is also preoccupied with the notion of the "burden" of the present, the terrifying freedom of the moment that comes from a recognition of the deceptiveness of time and brings to mind the frightening possibilities of action, particularly exacerbated in a world of collapsed values. As Lance pithily asks: "What do survivors do?" But in Lance's case, the burden of the present leads him to cast the "sinners" into eternity, and seek for himself a timeless Eden in Virginia. Finally, in *Lancelot*, the Percyean theme of the quest for God, or at least for signs of His presence, is turned into a perverse *via negativa* by which Lance searches for the Unholy Grail of sin to give meaning to his existence. The search fails, with disastrous consequences.

Percy's self-reflexive treatment of these themes in *Lancelot* is not, I think, simply a matter of the author attempting to stay one step ahead of his critics and readers. Rather, this fictional transformation of several of his own themes—*particularly* since the point of view is Lance's, an unrelenting and self-justifing moralist—suggests a deep questioning of the author's role as a moralist, as one of the judges who perhaps like Camus came to see the evil of judgement.

Yet if Lance Lamar is Percy's self-critical projection of that side of himself which acted as a condemning judge, and if on that level Lance is a projection of the possibilities of authorial "bad faith"—the author who stands imperiously outside of and above his world in order to condemn it—then this is only part of the story in *Lancelot*. To understand how Percy confronted this deep-seeded judgemental passion in his nature, we can return again fruitfully to the novel's intricate engagement with the themes and form of Camus's *The Fall*. In this way we can see how Percy's responses to the theological issues posed in *The Fall* are reflected by crucial differences in the form of the two novels. Percy had serious difficulties in constructing his novel, first trying to write it as a dialogue between Lance Lamar and his friend Percival/Fr. John. Only after a long struggle did he hit upon the idea of using the dramatic monologue as Camus had done in *The Fall*. But in that discovery he also found a way to move beyond the solipsistic and isolated condition which is the final plight of Camus's narrator. He discovered a way to both address the theological issues posed by Camus's novel, and to counterbalance the destructive passion for judgement he projected so extremely in Lance's diatribes. The two challenges—formal and thematic—essentially became one and the same, and I believe in confronting them Percy like Camus faced the most disturbing elements in his identity as a writer.

The crucial difference in form between *The Fall* and *Lancelot* is of course in the status and role of the listener. In Camus's novel the listener is basically a passive, silent audience to Clamence's monologue. Although himself a lawyer, he does not seriously question or challenge Clamence's interpretation of experience. In fact, the entire monologue insidiously traps the listener within Clamence's world of universal, unrelieved guilt, while Clamence himself maneuvers for a position of ascendency in this world through his role as judge-penitent. In this world understanding replaces mercy as the prime virtue. Clamence's listener never speaks directly in the novel; he has almost no real identity or force as a character beyond that of a narrative device to focus Clamence's monologue. Nor does Clamence's listener change during the course of the novel. More importantly, since he does not speak directly it cannot be said that a genuine bond of communication is established between the listener and Clamence. No real *community* is formed between the two individuals, and at the end of the novel the listener is preparing to leave. Clamence will again be alone until he beguiles another listener. We are left with the closed-world vision of Clamence at the end—a world of universal guilt over which he presides and judges before a silent, passive witness. Clamence's total absorption of the narrative is the technical manifestation of the all-consuming closure of his vision. In writing the *The Fall* Camus may well have taken the measure of his own "bad faith" as a judge, as Girard demonstrates, but in the end he still affirms the tragedy of a world of inescapable deceit and self-deception, a world unmediated by divine grace, where the dove of the Holy Spirit—the medium of charity—does not decent.

Percy's creation of the role of the listener in *Lancelot* is radically different. Like Clamence's listener, Fr. John is silent for the reader throughout most of the novel, speaking directly only at the end. But Fr. John does speak to Lance within the narrative, and he is an active, questioning and adversarial counterfoil to Lance's judgemental vision. Clamence's fall brought him the horrifying self-knowledge and admission of his own egotism and self-deceit, and such knowledge is the essence of the "hell" he now inhabits. Lance Lamar has yet to reach such a level of self-knowledge, and it is Fr. John's continuing struggle to bring his friend to such awareness.

What value is implicit in Percy's creation of Fr. John as a largely "silent" listener? If Girard's reading of Camus is correct, we can see that an author' shattering discovery of his own "bad faith" in being an "innocent" judge, coupled with a realization of the inherent duplicity of language, may well lead to the paralysis of solipsism or silence. But an author cannot be responsible and remain silent; both Camus and Percy were aware of this. So in *Lancelot* Percy's solution was to use Fr. John's silence as an active metaphor for charity, for *caritas*. Fr. John is the man who *refuses* to judge, who probes Lance with questions about love, who registers pain in suffering *with* Lance's delusions, who deeply respects the mystery of evil he faces in his friend Lance's present condition, yet who chooses a different vision of the world, and does not openly condemn. In the loving characterization of Fr. John, Percy found one way to answer the problem of judgement. Was it not personal a well as vocational?

Percy's deepening of the complexity of *Lancelot* as an exploration of his own motives is embedded in the Lance—Fr. John relationship. And to comprehend fully the layers of paradox, we must recognize the partial rightness of Lance's condemnation of the culture, yet also see how such condemnations challenge Fr. John's faith and, to a degree, *serve to reawaken it*. The lapsed priest's journey into the "hell" of unrelenting judgement (voiced by Lance) severely tests his faith, as indeed it must have tested Percy's. Yet it mysteriously enables him to witness to it in the face of the worst that Lance can charge against it—that Christianity is degraded, powerless, and irrelevant in a modern world saturated with corruption.

In *The Fall* Clamence attempts to evade judgement by assuming the duplicitous role of judge-penitent. His supposed penitence is of course a mask behind which he continues to judge mercilessly. In *Lancelot* Percy divided the role of judge-penitent between his two protagonists. Lance is the unrelenting judge and condemner, while Fr. John is the true penitent who recognizes his own sins as an offense against a God who can forgive him. And even though he is technically "silent" throughout much of the novel, Fr. John forms a genuine bond of community with Lance, unlike Clamence's listener. Fr. John and Lance truly communicate as equals by gesture, action, and word; theirs is not the relationship of ascendent, all-consuming voice and passive listener we find in Camus's novel. And their community and communication are left open-ended on the novel's last page, a metaphor for the hope implicit in Fr. John's (and Percy's) vision, an openness and hope radically different from the condition of existential closure in Clamence's sterile world at the end of *The Fall*.

In re-visioning the vision of judgement in *The Fall*, Percy staked everything on the transforming presence of the listener, Fr. John, and the radical change he undergoes. In contrast to Clamence's listener, Fr. John undergoes a radical change in the course of the novel. When the novel opens we discover him in the midst of his own spiritual crisis. His vocation as a missionary has failed; he has refused to pray for the dead in the cemetery; and he may be ready to abandon the priesthood altogether. But as the novel progresses, goaded by Lance's challenge, he reassumes his priestly garb, becomes more deeply committed as a spiritual counselor to Lance, and by the end of the novel he has decided to serve in a small parish in Alabama administering the sacraments to ordinary believers in the ordinary fallen world. No flight to a mythical Eden for him. Not only is Percy's listener transformed during the course of the novel, but his presence and involvement with Lance offer a glimmer of hope that the half-mad narrator may yet find a way out of his infernal prison of judgement—the way of *caritas* incarnated in the sacraments of grace dispensed by Fr. John. Clamence's listener has little to offer beyond resignation and understanding. Percy's listener offers a new world. Clamence calls himself "an empty prophet for shabby times . . . living in a desert of stones, fogs, and stagnant waters . . ." (117), "a false prophet crying in the wilderness and refusing to come forth" (147). In this mock identification with St. John, Clamence is the sterile precursor of an unredeemable world. But Percy's Fr. John is a true avatar of his namesakes, the precursor of Christ and the apostle of love, a genuine prophet who comes forth to live with hope in the modern wilderness.

The touchstone of the difference between the two novels is embedded in their contrary views of the meaning of Christ's crucifixion. For Clamence Jesus accepted death because of his consciousness of his own guilt for the massacre of the Holy Innocents. On the cross He rebelled against the Father for forsaking him. "It was better to have done with it (Clamence asserts), not to defend himself, to die in order not to be the only one to live, and to go elsewhere where perhaps he would be upheld" (113). Nevertheless, Clamence believes "He was not upheld. . . . And he was not superhuman. . . . He cried aloud his agony and that's why I love him, my friend who died without knowing" (116). Jesus dies, according to Clamence, without knowing the ultimate meaning of his fate, as a victim who wanted only to love and who refused to judge the adultress. Yet for Clamence Jesus's death is completely ineffectual. We continue to judge in his name, and "no one is ever acquitted anymore . . ." because "we are all judges, we are all guilty before one another, all Christs in our own mean manner, one by one crucified, always without knowing" (116).

Clamence's vision is a powerful humanistic reading of Jesus's life and death, but one that totally rationalizes the New Testament to strip it of mystery—mystery which is essential to belief. Clamence stresses Jesus's cry of abandonment to his Father, yet ignores Jesus's final acceptance—in mystery—of his

Father's will. Mystery is completely irrational to Clamence because it transcends human comprehension, and a life without full human comprehension—a life of faith—is for him an absurdity. Clamence likewise rationalizes the massacre of the Holy Innocents in order to impute guilt to a Jesus who cannot in his view be the incarnate Son of God. In doing so he holds Jesus responsible for human evil, as though it were Jesus and not Herod's soldiers who weilded the swords against the Innocents. Yet the massacred children were not "innocent" or exempt from the fallen condition. What Clamence really objects to (like Lance) is the fall itself. His real target is God and the human condition, just as Lance blames God for our sexual nature. What Clamence refuses to entertain is the mystery of how the suffering and death of the children may be the means of *their* salvation, through the suffering, death, and resurrection of the one in whose name they died. That somehow a God might send His only Son to reveal a way to overcome the evil manifested in the murder of the Innocents by the Son's death and resurrection is a mystery completely incomprehensible to Clamence.

Percy's listener, Fr. John, on the other hand, willingly embraces this mystery in his reawakened vocation as priest. In assuming this role and administering the sacraments he witnesses in hope to the scandal (Clamence would say "absurdity") of the divine presence in the ordinary, and to the reality of the transforming power of grace. And in his role as Lance's counselor, as one who is finally ready to speak to his friend at the end of the novel (perhaps like his creator to tell him what he needs to know in order to live), Fr. John suffers through the mystery of evil represented in Lance's situation and in his own spiritual dereliction, a mystery neither of the judges—Lance and Clamence—could accept without anguished rationalization. In so doing Fr. John follows the path of the God-man who not only refused to judge the adultress but also said, incomprehensibly, "Love your enemies. Do good to those who persecute you." The way Fr. John discovers is not that of a judge-penitent who stands outside or above the fallen community, waiting for the doves to descent, but back into the community, with hope and faith that judgement can be transfigured by mercy and love.

Camus's *The Fall* posed a challenge to Percy that was at once theological, vocational, and I believe personal. Like Girard in his view of *The Fall*, I have maintained that *Lancelot* is a work of profound self-criticism, one that dramatizes Percy's own wrestling with his passion for judgement and self-vindication, and his impulse toward charity, so intrinsic to his identity as an author. Percy's response to the theological problems posed by Camus's novel is, as we have seen, bound up with the technical strategy he devised in *Lancelot*, the development of the role of the listener that went far beyond the role of Clamence's listener in *The Fall*. The strategy, I believe, also gave Percy a way to confront the mystery of his own vocation as a writer—as one who judges, must judge, and yet must avoid the damning effects of a pride which, as Girard points out, "as it condemns others, unwittingly condemns itself" (34).

How is this so?

In creating Fr. John, Percy embodied in his listener that humility before creation, that humble and loving commitment to the ordinary things of the world, and especially humility before the mystery of evil, which the writer himself must finally attain in order not to succumb to the pharisaism of judgment as Clamence and Lance do, in order to witness in hope to *this* creation. Often in his interviews and essays Percy emphasized the "little way" of the writer, the loving attentiveness to the ordinary. In this he was aware that the demands of his vocation were finally co-extensive with the demands of his existence as a human being. For in constructing *Lancelot* Percy dramatized the insight that Camus himself expressed in his Nobel Prize speech: "Art . . . compels . . . the artist not to isolate himself; it submits him to the most humble and most universal truth. And he who, often, has chosen his artistic destiny because he considered himself different, learns rather quickly that he will only nourish his art, and his difference, by acknowledging his resemblance with others." By incarnating those demands—and hopes—in the person of Fr. John, Percy moved beyond the vision of *The Fall*, perhaps in more ways than one.

Notes

[1] Lawson, Lewis A. and Victor A. Kramer, ed. *Conversations with Walker Percy*. Jackson: University of Mississippi, 1985, p. 146.

[2] For a stimulating discussion of Camus's influence on Percy, see Phillip H. Rheim's "Camus and Percy: an acknowledged influence," in *Albert Camus:*

1980, ed. by Raymond Gay-Crosier. Gainesville: University Presses of Florida, 1980, pp. 257-265.

[3] Girard, Rene. "Camus's Stranger Retried," PMLA 79 (December 1964), pp. 519-533. My essay is greatly indebted to Girard's brilliant reading of *The Fall*.

[4] Camus, Albert. *The Fall*. New York: Vintage Books, 1956, epigraph. All further references to this edition.

[5] Percy, Walker. *Lancelot*. New York: Avon Books, 1977, pp. 235-236. All further references to this edition.

[6] Tolson, Jay. *Pilgrim in the Ruins: A Life of Walker Percy*. New York: Simon and Shuster, 1992, p. 300.

[7] Percy, Walker, "Questions They Never Asked Me," in *Signposts in a Strange Land*, ed. by Patrick Samway. New York: Farrar, Straus and Giroux, 1991, pp. 397-410 passim.

Signs of the Times:
Lancelot and the Misfit

A major study of the literary relationship between Flannery O'Connor and Walker Percy as regards the Catholic writer in the modern South has yet to be written. Nevertheless, there is enough evidence from Percy's writings and statements to indicate a strong affinity of vision between the two writers in spite of their considerable differences in sensibility and artistic technique. Percy's novels often echo O'Connor's ideas, as in his allusion to the theme of "the violent bear it away" in *The Second Coming,* or his extensive use of the theme that "tenderness leads to the gas chamber" in *The Thanatos Syndrome.* Percy's longer career as a writer obviously gave him a greater exposure to post-war American culture than O'Connor had; nevertheless, locating a similar core of beliefs and responses to modernity in both writers is still possible. Different aspects of this core echo throughout many of their works, but perhaps the most clearly evident is in O'Connor's and Percy's portrayals of two prophetic anti-heroes—The Misfit in "A Good Man Is Hard To Find" and Lancelot Lamar in *Lancelot.*

Although separated widely by social class, education, and intellectual sophistication, Lance and the Misfit share a similar philosophical position concerning the alternatives of belief and action available to "post-Christian" man. I would call this position an "either/or" philosophy. During his long monologue to Fr. John, Lance argues that the stark alternatives open to men and women are either a serious commitment to belief in Christ or capitulation to the hedonism and violence of contemporary Western society. "It will be your way or it will be my way," Lance tells Fr. John.[1] While Lance claims to reject "their way," the destructive self-indulgence of paganized Americans, his own "way" of forming a new society based on stoic virtues is, in fact only a more sophisticated version of that paganism. In Lance's new society, violence is sanctioned as a test of manhood, and his code of "honor"—which involves classifying women as either ladies or whores and treating them accordingly—is only a more formalized version of the hypocritical and dehumanizing behavior Lance condemns in hedonistic America. The philosophical foundation of both views is the same; both are based upon a totally secular view of the self.

Like Lance, O'Connor's Misfit has already come to believe that the alternatives are either commitment to Christ, or to autonomous self-sufficiency and violence:

> 'Jesus was the only one that ever raise the dead,' the Misfit continued, 'and He shouldn't have done it. He thown everything off balance. If He did what he said, then it's nothing for you to do but thow away everything and follow Him, and if He didn't, then it's nothing for you to do but enjoy the few minutes you got left the best way you can—by killing somebody or burning down his house or doing some other meanness to him. No pleasure but meanness.'[2]

What the Grandmother offers him as an alternative—that he might "settle down" and lead a comfortable life in society—is precisely the kind of vacuous, nominally Christian but in fact irreligious life that she lives and that Lance Lamar rejects in his tirades against decadent America. The Misfit intuits the bankruptcy of such an existence and chooses violence instead, aware like Dostoevski's hero that in a godless world "anything is possible."

The Misfit and Lance have reached such an extreme of alienation because, Percy believes, "the center did not hold"; that is, the old synthesis of nominal Christianity, secular humanism, and technological progress has collapsed in the twentieth century. The collapse of this synthesis issues in "the end of the modern world," a theme shared by O'Connor and Percy, both influenced by Romano Guardini's seminal work *The End of the Modern World*.[3] This shared apocalyptic sense—not the apocalypse to come but the one that has occurred—distinguishes them as religious writers from almost all other post-1950 Southern writers. Central to this apocalyptic view is a sense of the collapse of the ethical dimension of the Judeo-Christian/humanism synthesis. For humanity, the ethical realm is the crossroads between the bestial and the religious, the locus of genuine moral order. But O'Connor's and Percy's depictions of modern society reveal confusion, hypocrisy, and bankruptcy instead of a sustained moral order. The grandmother, whose unctious moral platitudes about "goodness" mask her smug elitism, represents such a hypocritical general condition, while Percy's Lance rails against the moral dereliction he sees beneath the veneer of social "niceness." Both the Misfit and Lance bear to some extent the mark of the prophet in their ability to detect the ethical vacuum that exists, and their prophetic power adds complexity to their status as heroes. Although both are deeply flawed, as seers they share a higher religious view of reality and reject the moral hypocrisy they see around them. Yet paradoxically, the moral bankruptcy they witness to is precisely what drives them to extremes of thought and action. Their violence, therefore, cannot be easily categorized and judged according to a conventional ethical standard; it is also a sign of a spiritual desperation that reveals their deepest longings for the religious. They exist in a situation that makes for killers—or saints. Moreover, the extremism of the Misfit and Lance shatters the quotidian calm of the status quo and reasserts the human desire for authenticity.

Both the Misfit and Lance know they inhabit a morally decadent society and neither is comfortable or acquiescent in the knowledge. Yet both reject belief in the mystery of the Christian redemption, while insisting upon the "either/or" nature of their predicament. Both try to save themselves by constructing autonomous, seemingly "rational" codes of ethics to give some sense to their experience; and both attempts fail. The Misfit now insists upon signed papers to verify his actions: ". . . Then you'll know what you done and you can hold up the crime to the punishment and see do they match and in the end you'll have something to prove you ain't been treated right" (131). But this rationalized code of "justice" cannot answer for or allay the deep sense of original sin and guilt he feels: "I call myself the Misfit . . . because I can't make what all I done wrong fit what all I gone through in punishment" (131). Neither can he make his code of "justice" answer logically for the violence he continues to practice, in spite of his good manners. For his part, Lance constructs a "rational" plan for a new society in Virginia, one based on a so-called ethical code of honor and justice. But like the Misfit's code, Lance's code fails to account for the mystery and contradiction that is at the heart of his own character—religious impulse coupled with demonic violence, "rational" ethic joined to irrational behavior.

The actions of both the Misfit and Lance represent conspicuous features of the times. Because of the conflict between their desire for rational order and meaning on the one hand, and the deeper, non-rational sources of their own being on the other (a contradiction they do not understand), violent action becomes their means of affirming a sense of identity. But such violence is inherently reductive of the self; it is cyclical in nature and literally self-defeating. More importantly, the Misfit's and Lance's attempts to construct an autonomous "rational" code of conduct are really attempts to recover a state of mock innocence *on their own terms*. The Misfit's desire for a strictly quantifiable justice actually betrays a longing for escape from the mystery of his own sense of himself as a fallen being. Likewise, Lance's plan for a new colony in Virginia reveals a desire to escape from the moral ambiguities of the human situation *per se*. But both of these attempts to reclaim mock innocence represent a flight from *actual* fallen history, a fact shown poignantly in the Misfit's murder of the grandmother precisely when she touches him and thereby claims a bond with him. To accept the bond implied in her remark—"Why you're one of my own babies"—would mean acknowledging a "connection" to fallen humanity. Instead, the Misfit uses violence in an attempt, as it were, to "recover" his innocence, as in a sense does Lance in purging his house with murder and fire. Significantly, he wants to take with him to Virginia the rape victim Anna, a woman he claims has recovered her innocence through violation. In this attempt to reject history and recover innocence by themselves both the Misfit and Lance have refused that sacrificial act of atonement already accomplished in history—Christ's redemption. In renouncing Christ, then, both assume the role of self-savior and prophet, yet warped prophets who are themselves signs of their age's spiritual dilemmas.

This false attempt to recover innocence is part of a larger theme shared by O'Connor and Percy—their strong distaste for sentimentality and its corrolary, the obscene. Sentimentality comes in for strong attack in "A Good Man Is Hard To Find" and *Lancelot*, and the basis of the attack is a theological conception of man and history. O'Connor satirizes the grandmother's nostalgic attachment to a fictitious Old South and to a hollow code of good manners, both of which are ruthlessly undercut with the Misfit's violence. As O'Connor noted in "The Church and the Fiction Writer," sentimentality involves a longing for lost

innocence, release from the suffering inherent in the fallen human state. Her famous statement about the Manichean temper
of many modern readers points to this defective sensibility:

> By separating nature and grace as much as possible, he
> has reduced his conception of the supernatural to pious
> cliches and has become able to recognize nature in liter-
> ature in only two forms, the sentimental and the ob-
> scene. He would seem to prefer the former, while being
> more of an authority on the latter, but the similarity
> between the two generally escapes him. He forgets
> that sentimentality is an excess, a distortion of senti-
> ment usually in the direction of an overemphasis on in-
> nocence, and that innocence, whenever it is overempha-
> sized in the ordinary human condition, tends by some
> natural law to become its opposite. We lost our inno-
> cence in the Fall, and our return to it is through the Re-
> demption which was brought about by Christ's death
> and by our slow participation in it. Sentimentality is a
> skipping of this process in its concrete reality and an
> early arrival at a mock state of innocence, which
> strongly suggests its opposite. Pornography, on the
> other hand, is essentially sentimental, for it leaves out
> the connection of sex with its hard purposes, and so far
> disconnects it from its meaning in life as to make it sim-
> ply an experience for its own sake.[4]

O'Connor's statement pinpoints the essentially anti-Christian, a-
historical core of sentimentality and pornography—their "innocence"—as well as their escapist character. In *Lancelot*, the sentimental and the pornographic are linked implicitly through the
motif of movie-making. The whole phony enterprise of depicting the Old South in a Hollywood film is ridiculed by Percy as a
ludicrous exercise in sentimentality and ignorance of history.
Yet Lance himself becomes a maker of pornographic films in an
attempt to "verify" the infidelities of his wife Margot. Lance's attempt at "verification" of the spiritual through technology is
both pornographic and sentimental because it denies the concrete mystery—and historicity—of Margot's being. His attempt
to verify Margot's infidelity becomes part of his proclaimed
larger quest to unravel the mystery of evil; yet this too is fueled
by sentimentality. Lance does not see that his quest is based
upon a false presumption of his own innocence, his belief that
he is merely the wronged husband; he ignores the fact that he is
also partly responsible for the failure of their marriage. Moreover, the very idea that one could empirically unravel the mystery of evil reveals Lance's hubristic naivete about reality, a

naivete rooted in his own sentimental unwillingness to accept evil as evil, especially the duplicity of his parents. Small wonder then that his search produces the logical counterpart of the sentimental—pornographic films of the *menage a trois* between his daughter Lucy, Raine, and Dana, and of the sexual antics of Margot and Jacoby. And Lance "enters the picture" with his own obscene violation of the drugged Raine.

Both the Misfit and Lance would appear to be anti-sentimentalists—cold, calculating agents who murder with planned precision and without remorse. Yet beneath the surface of their dispassionate behavior lies a sentimental core. Kierkegaard identifies sentimentality as an impulse toward the fantastic and as such, an impulse that seduces man away from his true self in the here-and-now, even to the point of an almost total loss of the self:

> Generally, the fantastical is that which so carries a man out into the infinite that it merely carries him away from himself and therewith prevent him from returning to himself.
> So when feeling becomes fantastic, the self is simply volatized more and more, at last becoming a sort of abstract sentimentality which is so inhuman that it does not apply to any person, but inhumanly participates feelingly, so to speak in the fate on one or another abstraction. . . .[5]

Such a fantastic sentiment underlies Lance's dream of creating a purified New Eden in Virginia to escape the here-and-now of history into a mythical future. A similar sentimental impulse underlies the Misfit's fantastic effort to create a personal world of "justice" completely cleansed of moral ambiguity, where he can hold deeds up to consequences to determine unequivocally if he has been treated right. Such a world can exist only in the nowhere of his mind, not in the real here-and-now of experience.

In both cases this fantastic impulse is rooted in the character's denial of the notion of a divine being entering history to transform the here-and-now without rejecting it. Both are attempts at mock transcendence initiated by mock saviors. And there is self-pity at the core of both characters' sentimentality, the sense of having been initially wronged by life before they had a chance to defend themselves. For Lance it is the betrayal he feels because of his parents' transgressions; for the Misfit it is the sense of having "gotten started wrong" before he could account logically for his actions. Yet the potential truer selves of the Misfit and Lance are also hinted at in their stories, particularly in their continuing links to the fallen community: Lance's link to Percival/Fr. John, and the Misfit's disgruntled final recognition that even his belief in "no pleasure but meanness" is unsatisfying. "It's no real pleasure in life," he tells Bobby Lee after shooting the grandmother. The cloud of the fantastic dissolves before the real.

In their sentimental escapism both the Misfit and Lance are revealed as victims of a despair that their creators see as pervasive in modern society. Despair, in Kierkegaard's well-known formulation in *The Sickness Unto Death*, means not to be a "true self," not to locate one's identity "transparently under God" (163). Despair is spiritual and grounded in the fact that man has a relation to himself that he "cannot get rid of" because the self is eternal (150). Both Lance and the Misfit try to "get rid of" their true, dependent selves by fantastic efforts at self re-definition. Their attacks are ultimately not against society but against their human condition in relation to God. As Kierkegaard says of the one who despairs:

> That self which he despairingly wills to be is a self which he is not (for to will to be that self which one truly is, is indeed the opposite of despair); what he really wills is to tear his self away from the Power which constituted it. But notwithstanding all his despair, this he is unable to do, notwithstanding all the efforts of despair, that Power is stronger, and it compels him to be the self he does not will to be. But for all that he wills to be rid of himself, to be rid of the self which he is, in order to be the self he himself has chanced to choose. To be *self* as he wills to be would be his delight (though in another sense it would be equally in despair), but to be compelled to be *self* as he does not will to be is his torment, namely, that he cannot get rid of himself. (153)

Though the Misfit and Lance suffer under despair, that condition is also the ground for hope, a paradox that accounts in part I believe for their subversive appeal as modern anti-heroes. According to Kierkegaard, the person who becomes conscious of his despair is a dialectical step closer to being cured than one who is unconscious of it. Although the Misfit and Lance do not explicitly acknowledge their despair, their rejection of the "security, the contentment of life" epitomized by the Grandmother and by Lance's society in general, and their intuition—seen in their mutual search for ultimate meaning—that they are fundamentally spiritual beings clearly imply that they have reached in the dialectic of despair a stage of consciousness where a reversal, or conversion, is entirely possible. The intensity of despair increases with an increase in consciousness, and by the end of their tales both the Misfit and Lance have evolved into a more intense awareness of their despairing condition, grounds for *metanoia*. In fact, for Kierkegaard the "gain of infinity," the awareness of oneself as spirit, "is never attained except through despair" (160). O'Connor argues that the Misfit may turn "into the prophet he was meant to become" (113). Percy leaves Lance open to the words of Fr. John at the end of *Lancelot*. Both the Misfit and Lance recognize that a social "center" founded upon hypocritical allegiance to a so-called "Christian" humanism will not hold, that indeed the violent will bear it away. But their hope—and the hope of society—is paradoxically in its despair. As Romano Guardini said of the modern age:

> The surrounding 'Christian' culture and the traditions supporting it will lose their effectiveness. . . . Loneliness in faith will be terrible. Love will disappear from the face of the public world (Matt., XXIII, 12), but the more precious will be that love which flows from one lonely person to another, involving a courage of the heart born from the immediacy of the love of God as it was made known in Christ. (132)

Notes

1 Percy, Walker. *Lancelot*. New York: Avon Publishing, 1977, p. 278. All further references are cited in the text.

2 O'Connor, Flannery. *The Complete Stories*. New York: Farrar, Straus and Giroux, 1971, p. 132. All further references are cited in the text.

3 Guardini, Romano. *The End of the Modern World*. Chicago: Henry Regnery Company, 1956, pp. 114-133 passim. All further references are cited in the text.

4 O'Connor, Flannery. *Mystery and Manners*. Ed. by Sally and Robert Fitzgerald. New York: Farrar, Straus and Giroux, 1959, pp. 147-148.

5 Kierkegaard, Soren. *Fear and Trembling* and *The Sickness Unto Death*. Garden City, NY: Doubleday Anchor Books, 1941, 1954, p. 164. All further references are cited in the text.

Walker Percy, Flannery O'Connor, and the Holocaust

Readers of Walker Percy's last novel, *The Thanatos Syndrome*, recognize an obvious similarity between his character Fr. Rinaldo Smith's argument about the significance of the Holocaust and that of Flannery O'Connor in her introduction to *A Memoir of Mary Ann*. In the latter work, O'Connor saw the Holocaust as a horrifying example of modern sentimentality, which she in turn recognized as rooted in an ethic of tenderness that is divorced from the meaning of Christian redemption.

> Ivan Karamazov cannot believe, as long as one child is in torment; Camus' hero cannot accept the divinity of Christ, because of the massacre of the innocent. In this popular pity, we mark our gain in sensibility and our loss in vision. If other ages felt less, they saw more, even though they saw with the blind, prophetical, unsentimental eye of acceptance, which is to say, of faith. In the absence of this faith now, we govern by tenderness. It is a tenderness which, long since cut off from the person of Christ, is wrapped in theory. When tenderness is detached from the source of tenderness, its logical outcome is terror. It ends in forced labor camps and in the fumes of the gas chamber.[1]

O'Connor distinguished this sentimental "tenderness" from true compassion, which she defined elsewhere as "the sense of being in travail with and for creation in its subjection to vanity."[2] Compassion for her is not a theoretical pity; it is concrete, which is to say it is historical, and it is linked to a historical process which involves suffering but also creative action in the real fallen world. In other words, genuine tenderness or compassion is rooted in a view of creation that is centered upon Christian redemption; whereas modern tenderness, "wrapped in theory," represented for her an escape from the hard yet accepting truth of the Christian vision. (To be "in travail" with creation is to identify with the evolutionary process leading to the ultimate fulfillment of the Divine Plan). O'Connor elaborated on this in a comment about the modern reader's attraction to the sentimental and the obscene in literature. Such a reader, O'Connor argued

> . . . forgets that sentimentality is an excess, a distortion of sentiment usually in the direction of an overemphasis on innocence, and that innocence, whenever it is over-emphasized in the ordinary human condition, tends by some natural law to become its opposite. We lost our innocence in the Fall, and our return to it is through the Redemption which was brought about by Christ's death and by our slow participation in it. Sentimentality is a skipping of this process in its concrete reality and an early arrival at a mock state of innocence, which strongly suggests its opposite. Pornography, on the other hand, is essentially sentimental, for it leaves out the connection of sex with its hard purpose, and so far disconnects it from its meaning in life as to make it simply an experience for its own sake.[3]

What is clear from O'Connor's remark is her belief that a genuine concept of compassion is inseparable from the person of Christ and the specific historical event of His incarnation, death, and resurrection. The Redemption is that pivotal event in history which defines and validates the ultimate spiritual worth of every individual. Modern sentimental "tenderness," on the other hand, is abstract and ahistorical; it looks upon the individual person in terms of a humanly-constructed model or theory. Such a model may be idealistic *in the abstract*, but it masks a pride which implies both presumption and condescension. For when a specific individual—such as a Downes Syndrome child or a hopelessly senile geriatric—cannot or does not conform to the model or theory, then the thin mask of sentimentality is torn away to reveal contempt, a contempt which for O'Connor often issues in coercion, terror, and death.

Behind the mask of the abstract do-gooders, social reformers, and idealists—all mock saviors who would displace or ignore Christ—is the potential terrorist. For O'Connor, any idealism which is rooted solely in a secular ethic of pity is inherently flawed because man is flawed, and attempts to create a perfect social order based upon this ethic can eventuate in murder. Hence the gas chamber and forced labor camps are her prime examples of this abstract, anti-Christian ethic, since they deny on theoretical ground the intrinsic worth of the individual person.

In *The Thanatos Syndrome*, Walker Percy's character Fr. Smith delivers a long confession to his friend Dr. Tom More in which he recounts his experiences living in Germany before World War II and acknowledges that, had he remained there, he too would have joined the SS along with his friend Helmut Jager, son of the famous professor of psychiatry Dr. Hans Jager. Fr. Smith says that he was strongly attracted by the general decency, humaneness, and culture of the upper-class Germans, many of whom were Catholics. Later, however, while participating in the Allied liberation of Europe, Smith discovered to his horror that the eminent Dr. Jager was a key figure in the medical extermination of children during the war. Brooding over these events many years later, Fr. Smith now tells his friend More: "Tenderness leads to the gas chamber. . . . Tenderness is the first guise of the murderer."[4]

The immediate cause of Fr. Smith's brooding is the direct parallel he sees between the presumptuous, abstract cultural ideal of racial purity behind which the Nazis perpetrated mass exterminations and a similar abstract ideal of social "purification" used by Dr. More's colleagues to justify their plans for euthanasia and coercion by drugs. The language Percy uses in Fr. Smith's argument—that "tenderness leads to the gas chambers"—echoes that of Flannery O'Connor quite closely, of course, although Percy once said in an interview that he was not aware of how his language echoed O'Connor's. Moreover, the fact that the corrolary plot to the euthanasia/coercion by drugs scheme in the novel concerns Dr. More's attempt to save children from pedophiles who practice pornography suggests a strong similarity to O'Connor's argument about the relationship between sentimentality, "mock tenderness," and pornography quoted above. Percy's debt may be directly to O'Connor, but even if this is not the case, what is most important is that Fr. Smith's viewpoint on tenderness is rooted in the same belief in Christ and his Redemption as O'Connor's is. However, in *The Thanatos Syndrome* Percy's treatment of the subject is more expansive. Through Fr. Smith's experience of the Holocaust, Percy develops a long meditation on the meaning of the Jews in the history of the West by linking it to his theory of language. By connecting these themes Fr. Smith is able to speak prophetically about the present state of Christianity in our culture.

This link between the Jewish experience in history, the Holocaust, modern Christianity, and language is developed explicitly in another conversation between Fr. Smith and Dr. More. Echoing a persistent Percyean theme, Fr. Smith insists that words no longer signify the reality they are supposed to name; they have become "emptied of meaning" (359). The priest tells Dr. More that Satan is the cause of this disjunction between word-sign and reality; Satan is the "depriver of meanings" (359). To demonstrate how language is devalued, Fr. Smith uses as analogy the technique of triangulating coordinates to pinpoint the location of fires from his fire tower retreat. A single coordinate on the sign of fire—smoke—is inadequate; the accurate location of the fire can only be determined by using a second coordinate, an "other" viewpoint which establishes communication and by which the truth of the sign can be verified. Fr. Smith's implication is clear: In the absence of the "other" coordinate to establish communication about the real, the sign is "empty," deprived of meaning. His analogy is a concrete example of the triadic theory of language Percy developed in great detail elsewhere, especially in *The Message in the Bottle* and in his central parable about language in *Lost in the Cosmos*.

Just as Fr. Smith names Satan specifically as the depriver of meaning, he implies also that the Godhead—the Divine Logos—is the ultimate source of naming and meaning. Moreover, since Christ's Incarnation means the entrance of the Divine Logos into human history, then Christ's Redemption becomes the focal point of triangulation, the historical coordinate or "sign," through which the historical process receives its transcendent meaning. This transcendent meaning of the Christ event is continued throughout history in one form through the sacraments, those "outward signs" of grace which communicate the divine power of redemption. Percy underscores this link by showing Fr. Smith repeatedly in relation to the Mass—the eucharistic sacrament—near the end of the novel, with Dr. More as his sometimes assistant.[5]

In addition to implying the Christian sacrament as a valid sign of God's communication to man, Percy also suggests the broader possibility of human communication and human love as a means of recovery from "devaluation." A joining of "coordinates," a linking of two human beings in a named bond of love, is possible. But here the problem of "tenderness" named by O'Connor and Fr. Smith arises again, because language contains not only the power to name truth but also a terrible capacity for deception and self-deception. All manner of atrocities and betrayal can be committed in the name of love, benevolence, and idealism. Fr. Smith has abandoned the world for his fire tower retreat in large part, Percy suggests, because he could not stand the pervasive atmosphere of deceit—of corrupt language—in modern culture. And when he returns to the world near the end of the novel to minister to terminal patients and other social outcasts, the priest insists that he likes them because the dying "do not lie"; their communication is rooted in openness and truth.

But the possibility of a human love that is genuinely respectful of the other and not corrupted by manipulation—linguistic or otherwise—must have a historical axis, a "coordinate" to give it definition and transcendent meaning. It must connect, as O'Connor suggested, with the true source of tenderness, Christ and the Christian belief in the intrinsic worth of the individual. To suggest this "coordinate" in *The Thanatos Syndrome* Fr. Smith gives Dr. More a second example of the problem of language deprived of meaning, one directly related to the meaning of the Jews in history. The priest gives Dr. More a free association word test in which More typically responds to each item by categorizing it into a larger generic group. But not in the case of the word "Jew," which triggers specific responses about specific Jews whom Dr. More knows.

> "Okay, Irish." (Fr. Smith says)
> "Bogs, Notre Dame, Pat O'Brien, begorra—"
> "Okay, Blacks."
> "Blacks?"
> "Negroes."
> "Blacks, Africa, Niggers, Minority, Civil Rights—"
> "Okay, Jew."
> "Israel, Bible, Max, Sam, Julius, Hebrew, Hebe, Ben—"
> "Don't you see?"
> "No."
> "Unlike the other test words, what you associated with the word *Jew* was Jews, Jews you have known."
> (121-122)

From this experiment Fr. Smith argues that Jews are "unsubsumable"; they are "the only sign of God that has not been evacuated by an evacuator." The unique particularity of the Jews is linked to their unique historical character. Redemption history begins with the Jews, and is defined by the Incarnation. Consequently, Smith argues that because the Jews are the original chosen people of God, the focus of salvation in history, they are an ineradicable sign of God's presence in the world, one that cannot be evacuated of meaning. Therefore, the attempt to exterminate the Jews in the Holocaust is implicitly an attempt to exterminate God, the True Signifier, from history.

Given this theological view of history, then, Fr. Smith sees the Holocaust as "a consequence of the sign which could not be evacuated" (126). The fact that the Jews as the chosen people are "unsubsumable" is an offense to many people, the priest argues, especially "people of the loftiest sentiments, the highest scientific achievements, and the purest humanitarian ideals" (126). Having rejected the Christian vision of history, these sentimental idealists appeal instead to a self-created myth of human perfectibility as a justification for action. Thus for Fr. Smith the "origins of the Holocaust are a myth—" (127). Dr. More seems to misunderstand the priest's point; he thinks Fr. Smith is referring to the fugitive notion that the Holocaust never really happened. "Are you telling me that the Nazis did not kill six million Jews?" he asks. "No," the priest replies. "They did kill six million Jews" (127).

What Percy is affirming through Fr. Smith's argument is a distinction between history and myth. Myth is a subsuming form; it subsumes individual character and actions into general categories, searching out archetypal patterns to classify into universal forms of behavior. History, in contrast, is radically individuated, and in the Christian vision its individual character is given its unique meaning by Christ's entrance into history, by His election of the Jews, and by the Christ event.[6] It is in this sense that Fr. Smith sees the Holocaust as originating in a myth, because it was rooted in a man-made, hubristic model of human personality, one that denied the true historical reality of mankind's fallen condition and Christ's redemption. As O'Connor stated, we now "govern by tenderness" wrapped *in theory*, but cut off from the person of Christ. Consequently, the myth of Aryan superiority is a perverse variant of the original myth of the perfectibility of man. It attempts to reverse the true history of the Fall, demonically, and its "logical" outcome is the gas chambers and the concentration camps.

In *The Thanatos Syndrome* this same kind of mythologizing is now being practiced by the high-minded social engineers and physicians who perform abortion, mercy-killing, and "behavior modification" by invoking an ideal of a more perfect society or greater "quality" of life. Having rejected the whole "Jewish-Christian thing," they now govern by pity. So Fr. Smith warns Dr. More that he and his fellow physicians will end up like the Nazis—killing Jews—because the Jews are an affront to the myth, and cannot be subsumed by it. The priest concludes his confession by telling More: "In the end you must choose, life or death" (122). It is in this sense of the meaning of the Jews and the Christ event as signs that I think we must see the meaning of Percy's title: *The Thanatos Syndrome*. A syndrome can be seen as a group of signs which collectively point to a disorder; so also the activities of Dr. More's colleagues are signs of a demonic impulse that empties reality and language of meaning and then promotes death by appeal to higher claims for enriching life.

For Flannery O'Connor and Walker Percy, the Holocaust exists as a stumbling block and a sign. It is a stumbling block to those secular idealists and believers in progress who cannot reconcile its truth—the grimmest recent example of the Fall of man—with their exalted vision of humanity, particularly since the Nazis used a central tool of the progressive ideology, technological power, to carry out their demonic plans. But for O'Connor and Percy the Holocaust is also the sign of a much greater drama being acted out in history, the drama of the struggle with evil, and the quest for eternal salvation. Both writers understood that the underlying struggle represented in the Holocaust was the age-old one against Satan, the "depriver of meaning," a struggle that continues today in more subtle guises. For them the central question raised by the Holocaust is neither social, political, or economic—but theological: What is a human being? And for O'Connor and Percy, the Jewish experience in history, and the Christ event which issues from it, are the unique clues to the answer to that question—the sign of salvation and indestructible hope for mankind.

Notes

[1] O'Connor, Flannery. Introduction to *A Memoir of Mary Ann*. New York: Dell Publishing Co., 1961.

[2] O'Connor, Flannery. "Novelist and Believer," in *Mystery and Manners*, ed. by Sally and Robert Fitzgerald. New York: Farrar, Straus and Giroux 1961.

3 O'Connor, Flannery. "The Church and the Fiction Writer," in *Mystery and Manners*, ed. by Sally and Robert Fitzgerald. New York: Farrar, Straus and Giroux, 1961, 147-148.

4 Percy, Walker. *The Thanatos Syndrome*. New York: Farrar, Straus and Giroux, 1987.

5 See Kathleen Scullen-Esser's "Connecting the Self with what is outside the Self," *Renascence*, XL, no. 2, Winter 1988, pp. 67-75 for an excellent discussion of the linguistic basis of Percy's triangulation of language and theme. Our discussions coincide on key points about the triangulation, though Scullen-Esser does not emphasize the sacraments, the deceptiveness of language, or the theme of tenderness in the way that I do.

6 See especially Mircea Eliade's *The Sacred and the Profane*. New York: Harcourt Brace and World, 1959, pp. 63-113.

Disjunctions of Time:
Myth and History in *The Thanatos Syndrome*

Readers of Walker Percy's *The Thanatos Syndrome* are by now familiar with the conscious parallels drawn between the spiritual ethos of pre-World War II Nazi Germany and that of Tom More's contemporary world in Feliciana parish, Louisiana. Resounding throughout Dr. More's struggle against the euthanasists of Fedville and the pedophiles at Belle Ame are echoes of the German medical world of the 1930's, and the parallel is made explicit by Fr. Rinaldo Smith. Moreover, Percy adds a third historical situation to this pattern when we discover that Dr. Comeaux and his associates have treated Negro criminals with heavy sodium to pacify them into "happy darkies" who sing spirituals while they work in the prison cotton fields. Since freedom and tyranny are major themes in the novel, Percy's strategy in this regard seems clear. By drawing conscious parallels between contemporary Feliciana, Nazi Germany, and a fake mythological vision of the ante-bellum slave world, Percy underscores the pattern of repetition in which humans are coerced into submission, rendered less than human, by either violent or subtle means of manipulation. Moreover, since each of these three situations is rooted in a mythological conception of events, a conception directly at odds with the Christian historical vision of reality, the paralleling also serves to raise deeper questions about the meaning of history and Tom More's responsible relationship to it.

While these parallels are fairly obvious, what is not so readily apparent I think is Percy's strategic use of disjunctions of time in the novel, especially as a formal device by which to chart the course of Tom More's development. More seems to be that relatively stable protagonist from whose viewpoint we observe the fugitive actions of other characters in the novel, and this is generally true. But More is also undergoing his own deep per-

sonal crisis, and by using the formal device of temporal disjunction in two crucial scenes—scenes intrinsically linked by image
and idea—Percy is able to unite Tom More's predicament to the
larger concerns about the relationship between myth and history. The two episodes I have in mind are Tom's journey to
Pantherburn where he is seduced by his "cousin" Lucy (133-186),
and Fr. Smith's confession to Tom and his Footnote to the confession (239-257).[1] Both episodes are formally "separated" from
the ongoing narrative of the story; yet they are separated in different ways, the significance of which I think will become clear.
And both episodes, as I noted, are intimately related to each
other by image and idea in such a way as to reveal Tom More's
struggle to exercise his own freedom to make crucial moral decisions.

More's visit to Pantherburn is a complicated episode that
unites a variety of important motifs in the novel. On one level
it is a journey into his past; Pantherburn evokes memories of his
earlier visits to the estate, as well as more distant family memories. On another level it is a journey of discovery about the present—through cousin Lucy's computer network they discover
the Blue Boy plot of drugging sections of Feliciana parish.
Equally important for More personally is his discovery of his
wife Ellen's apparent adultery with Van Dorn. John Edward
Hardy has also suggested a mythic level: More the knight
questor's journey to the dark castle, where he is tempted by
woman.[2] What should be emphasized in all this, it seems to
me, is that More's visit to Pantherburn is largely, though not entirely, a descent into despair, into a state of spiritual anomie
which is underscored by the formal disjunction of time during
much of the episode.[3] Nevertheless, this journey into despair is
ambiguously fruitful, because from it More is able to find a
clearer spiritual direction for himself, one that is confirmed in
the confession scene with Fr. Smith.

More's relationship to his "cousin" Lucy is a curious one,
to say the least. Their common ancestor, an English army officer, was also a bigamist, marrying a young American girl while
already married to an English wife. Later, this melancholy ancestor committed suicide by drowning. Lucy's connection is to
the English side of the family, Tom's to the American; so they
are "hardly kin at all" (136). Though Tom is old enough to be
Lucy's father, he sees her "more as a mother" and indeed,
throughout the episode, Lucy "mothers" him even to the point

of a symbolically incestuous seduction. What Percy creates throughout the episode on the psychological level is Tom's destructive regression to a narcissistic state, a kind of personal "thanatos" that More must struggle out if he is to act as a free moral agent.

The beginnings of this regressive journey are suggested in various ways. Lucy's persistent, telling gesture of "clicking thumbnail to tooth," her constant smoking of Picayunes, her mothering of Tom so that he "feels safe" at Pantherburn—all these images, like the "thumb-sucking" gestures of Raine and Lance in the rape/murder scenes in *Lancelot*, suggest that Tom is embarked upon a regression to childhood. Moreover, the visit to Pantherburn begins with Tom experiencing a *deju vu* as he sits with Lucy in his Chevrolet Caprice. It is a memory of "cars, women, girls, the past, the old U.S.A., about remembering what it was like to be sitting in a car with girl swiveled around to face you, her bare knee cocked upon the vinyl, with four wheels under you, free to go anywhere . . ." (106). This seemingly innocuous memory is in fact an important sign of the beginning of the confusion of Tom More's time sense, which becomes more extreme when he reaches Pantherburn.

What Percy is suggesting here in More's *deja vu* and his increasing disjunction from time is nothing less than a state of alienation from linear historical time as defined by the Judeo-Christian experience, and his entrapment in the cyclical repetition of mythic time. The distinction is made most clearly by Mircea Eliade:

> Compared with the archaic and paleo-oriental religions, as well as with the mythical-philosophical conceptions of the eternal return, as they are elaborated in India and Greece, Judaism presents an innovation of the first importance. For Judaism, time has a beginning and will have an end. The idea of cyclic time is left behind. Yahweh no longer manifests himself in *cosmic time* (like the gods of other religions) but in a *historical time*, which is irreversible. . . .
>
> Christianity goes even further in valorizing *historical time*. Since God was *incarnated*, that is, since he took on *a historically conditioned human existence*, history acquired the possibility of being sanctified. The *illus tempus* evoked by the Gospels is a clearly defined historical time—the time in which Pontius Pilate was Governor of Judea—but it was *sanctified by the presence of Christ*. When a Christian of our day

> participates in liturgical time, he recovers the *illus*
> *tempus* in which Christ lived, suffered, and rose
> again—but it is no longer a mythical time, it is the time
> when Pontius Pilate governed Judea. . . . (But we should
> add that, for the Christian, time begins anew with the
> birth of Christ, for the Incarnation establishes a new
> situation of man in the cosmos.) This is as much to say
> that history reveals itself to be a new dimension of the
> presence of God in the world. . . .[4]

In a slightly different manner, Percy made a similar distinction in response to a question about Will Barrett's mental state in *The Last Gentleman*, a distinction I believe equally applicable to Tom More at Pantherburn.

> His disorientation in time has to do with a theory of
> Professor Eric Voegelin's about two sense of time. In his
> book Voegelin contrasts the unhistoric cyclical time of
> the Greeks and Orientals with the historic linear time
> of Israel—historical time began when Israel emerged.
> Barrett's amnesia suggests a post-Christian shakiness
> about historic time.[5]

More's *deja vu*, his disjunction from time, then, indicates a state of mind struggling under a confusing bombardment of experiences—past and present, real and imaginary—that are separated from a *coherent* sense of the historical real which, Percy suggests later through Fr. Smith, derives from the Judeo-Christian experience. But at this point in the novel More is trapped in a mode of consciousness that is free-floating as regards historical time.

Nevertheless, Percy has More's journey to Pantherburn preceded by a strategically placed visit to Fr. Smith, during which the priest delivers his first lesson about the meaning of the Jews and the Holocaust. He also warns More about his involvement in the Fedville project. But at this point More doesn't "get" the historical connection Fr. Smith is trying to make between these events. More lacks both knowledge and a sense of personal complicity, two requisites which the trip to Pantherburn will ironically help to fulfill.

Once Tom arrives at Pantherburn his dangerous moral slide toward despair is suggested in several ways. Met immediately by Lucy, who gives him a "frank kiss" on the mouth, More experiences another *deja vu* triggered by the smell of her cotton shirt. His willpower slackens. "I know if I choose to know, but don't of course, what will happen next. And yet I do" (135). Attracted to Lucy as a woman, More begins to drink heavily, further weakening his resistance to this "mothering" comforter who wants to keep him to herself at Pantherburn. The house itself, of course, is a strong tie to the ante-bellum past, and the conversation between More, Lucy, and her uncle Hugh Bob while they drink evokes the old slave world. In this talk Percy again implicitly parallels the overt slavery of the 1830's and the covert slavery to drugs (including alcohol as well as heavy sodium) of the present. Percy also uses other echoes of the past to suggest More's incipient regression. He is to stay in the room of Lucy's ex-husband Dupre, a room once used by General Earl Van Dorn, a Civil War hero. Moreover, in his talk Lucy's uncle constantly romanticizes war and sexual license. He evokes the world of hunting, and he admires equally and without moral distinction three groups of fighters: the Romans, the Germans, and the Americans. All of these motifs associated with Hugh Bob suggest a world view based on the heroic mythos of stoicism and conquest, entirely anti-Christian.

More's slide toward despair continues while he and Lucy work together at the computer to uncover the Blue Boy drugging project. The scene is an odd but telling mixture of seduction on two levels—Tom and Lucy hunting to reveal the chemical "seduction" of his patients; Lucy at the same time working to seduce Tom. That this is the road to a kind of spiritual thanatos is underscored by another *deja vu* Tom has just before he gets the bitter knowledge of his wife's infidelity. "The tragic tingle of bad news. The sweet sorrow to come. It is like the touch of a friend at a funeral (156). Lucy *already knows* of Ellen's adultery, and has deceitfully withheld it from Tom until the most advantageous moment. Although Ellen's responsibility is qualified by the fact that she too has been drugged with heavy sodium, for Tom the news is devastating psychologically. Almost like a dead man he says "I don't feel anything," and then literally chases down his bitter knowledge with another cocktail and two Alanone, compliments of Lucy.

To emphasize the depth of More's despair *precisely* in relation to the larger theme of time, myth, and history, Percy formally breaks the continuity of the narrative with a disjointed series of reveries that culminate in More's seduction by Lucy. Thus the technique of disjunction replicates and reinforces More's moral "disjunction" or confusion. Ellen's act of adultery is then answered by his own, contrived by the "mother" figure Lucy.

Filled with the "sweet sorrow" of knowledge of Ellen's infidelity, More stands drinking at the sideboard in the dining
room while his mind wanders over the past.   He remembers
standing in the same spot "twenty years" ago, remembers exactly
where the decanter of Uncle Rylan's cheap bourbon was kept,
and the "child's silver cup" used for a jigger, which he now uses
again.   Drinking heavily, he begins to experience a free-floating
separation from time.

> It is not bad standing in the dark drinking.
> ----- ----- ----- ----- -----
> There is this to be said for drinking. *It frees one from
> the necessity of time*, like: now it is time to sit down,
> stand up. One would as soon do one thing as another.
> ----- ----- ----- ----- -----
> *Time passes*, but one need not tell oneself: take *heed*,
> *time is passing*. (159) (Italics mine)

More's separation from time, his drinking, his indulgent savor-
ing of the "sweet sorrow" of Ellen's fall, his childhood reveries
about Pantherburn—all combine to reinforce his despair.   "As a
child I associated the pleasure of doom with the tinkle of silver
against crystal" (160).   Sunk in anomie, More cannot even re-
spond when Lucy attempts to commiserate with him in his sorrow.

> 'I know how you feel.' says Lucy. 'Did you ever know
> how I felt about you?'
> 'No.'
> She's wrong. I don't feel anything but the bird-dog reek
> of memory. (160)

Nevertheless, More is alert enough to sense Lucy's connection
with the doom-ridden mythos of the Old South and the melancholy ancestor who committed suicide.   As Lucy leads him to
bed, he reflects: "They, the English Lipscombs, must have spoken
exactly the same way (as Lucy), with the same doomed convivi-
ality and the same steady tinkle of silver against crystal, when
the Americans came down the river two hundred years ago in
1796 and up the river with Silver Spoons Butler in 1862" (161).
   Once in bed, Tom's confusion about time and reality takes
its most bizarre turn, for when he recalls that it used to be a
"feather bed," his mind skips to a "memory" of a feather bed
with a bolster in Freiburg, and of waking in the morning to the
sound of church bells tolling.   This in turn triggers another
"memory" of a hike taken in his younger days in pre-war Germany with one Alice Pratt, a Southern girl to whom More was

attracted in this seemingly timeless romantic, youthful world
where they are ". . . caught, trapped between the happy, safe,
Weiner-waltz musical security of the Grand Tour of the 1870's
and the shacked-up stoned out ease of the 1970's" (162). Their
tryst in the Schwarzwald, filled with Tom's anxiety about
"touching" Alice Pratt, culminates romantically when there appears ". . . a Tiger tank leading a column of tanks, a Wehrmacht
officer standing in the open forward hatch" (162). Tom acts the
chauvinistic hero.

> I grab Alice Pratt and yank her into the dark fir forest.
> We lie in a soft bed of needles and watch an entire
> panzer division pass. I am Robert Jordan lying on the
> pine needles. I hold her. She wants me too. When the
> panzers are gone, we look at each other and laugh. We
> have been given leave by the German army and Robert
> Jordan. (163)

There is only one difficulty, as Tom later acknowledges: "I have
never been to Germany" (166). Yet Percy places this disjointed,
erroneous "memory," one that again connects Nazi Germany
with Old South romantic chivalry, *precisely* at the moment of
Lucy's seduction of Tom, his dazed mind "con-fusing" real and
fictitious events.

> Her mouth is on mine. She, Alabama-German-Lucy-
> Alice, is under the comforter and I under her, she a
> sweet heavy incubus but not quite centered. Her hair is
> still damp. She needs centering. (163)

An incubus, we recall, is an evil spirit which descends to mate
with sleeping women. Percy's inversion of the sexual roles here,
with Lucy dominant, underscores the extent of More's psychological and spiritual debility. A despairing cuckold, he now
submits passively to seduction by the "mothering" Lucy, who in
his mind becomes a figure emblematic of a romanticized Southern past and the doom-filled world of Nazi Germany. The symbolic connection is most telling, especially if we had any doubts
about the helpful intentions of incubus-Lucy. Her drugging of
Tom with bourbon and Alanone is only a more subtle version of
Fedville's drugging of patients with heavy sodium, equally as
destructive of conscious freedom. Life with her at Pantherburn
is a death for Tom both psychologically and spiritually, emphasized by the fact that his act of choice is badly crippled in his
submission to Lucy's wiles.

Again, through the technique of disjunction, Percy emphasizes the confused, atemporal, "mythic" consciousness that
dominates his hero at Pantherburn. Throughout the entire
episode of his adultery with Lucy, Tom's mind is saturated with
muddled "memories" of past and present, all dissociated from
any real time sense, hence without coherent order. For example,
he remembers things from the family Southern past: Grandmother Bett's journal, the distribution of slaves to the seven
Lipscomb brothers, Rylan Lipscomb's death in the Civil War,
memories of sleeping in the feather bed with the bolster, and of
Colley the Negro retainer making the fire in the grate. These
fragmented "memories" (some perhaps untrue) are fused with
others from More's past that link motifs of war, hunting, and
sexual license. For example, Tom recalls a fellow inmate in Fort
Pelham prison, Harry Epps, who knew a "dial-a-girl number in
Pensacola and how to get not a recording but a woman" (164).
The woman says, significantly, "Now why don't we both relax
and tell each other what we like. *I have all the time in the
world*" (my italics). More then recalls the perverse sexual habits
of a couple who visited him for marriage counseling, disjunction of another sort.

> He to her: I like the explicit VCR in the bedroom, in 3-
> D, and living color. We both get excited. You have to
> admit you do. Doc, you ought to hear her.
> She to him: Yes, but you're really screwing her not me.
> He to both of us: It's better than nothing, isn't it?
> I: (silent: flummoxed). (165)

And finally, More recalls the despairing "wisdom" of Lucy's uncle, that superannuated good-ole-boy Southerner, on war and
sex: "That's a lot of crap about war being hell . . . I never had a
better time in my life" (164). "And I'll tell you another thing
they're wrong about. A little pussy never hurt anybody" (165).

Yet the entire nightmare of drunkenness, mental confusion, and adultery ends for Tom with a crushing return to reality
in time present.

> I have never been to Germany.
> There is no coal fire in the grate.
> Colly has been dead for forty years.
> Miss Betts has been dead for fifty years, Aunt Bett for a
> hundred years.
> The uncle did not come in my room. The French windows
> are locked.

But now he is walking up and down the gallery calling
ducks.
There is a Picayune taste in my mouth. (166)

II.

I have never been to Germany. What, then, is the source
of Tom More's "memory" of awakening in a feather bed in
Freiburg to the sound of church bells, of hiking in the
Schwarzwald, and a romantic, Hemingwayesque tryst with Alice
Pratt, hiding from a Nazi Panzer division? More importantly,
what is the point of Percy's strategy, beyond showing the moral
and psychological confusion underlying More's tryst with Lucy
at Pantherburn? The clue is to be found, as I have suggested, in
the close connections drawn between the scene at Pantherburn
and Fr. Smith's confession about his German experience, delivered later in the novel. These connections are both technical
and thematic, and bear careful scrutiny.[6] Technically both the
episode of Tom's confused reverie and the priest's confession
are set off from the continuing narrative; Percy even gives the
Confession and the Footnote distinctive titles. But beyond this
similarity, the episodes are formally opposite in that Fr. Smith's
confession is a carefully ordered rendering of events, indicative
of a mind ordering and penetrating the past to understand it and
its meaning for the present. In this sense it is *not* disjoined from
historical time. This is also totally unlike More's confused
reveries at Pantherburn. What Percy has in mind, here, I think,
is to suggest by technique a progression in More's development
as he moves closer to the influence of the priest and away from
Lucy's influence, and as he moves both toward an ordering of
his own affairs and the assumption of his responsibility as doctor
to thwart the Blue Boy project and expose the pedophiles. As far
as theme is concerned, I believe Percy's correlating of the two
episodes is intended to illuminate the larger meaning of events
in the novel in terms of the relationship between myth and
history, mythical time and historical time. But that is to get
ahead of the story somewhat.

What initiates the episode that becomes Fr. Smith's confession is More's desire to seek advice from the priest about what
to do about the Blue Boy project. This is a key step in developing
an important kinship and mutual influence between the two
men. In fact, near the end of the novel, musing over Fr. Smith's

favorite theme about the emptying of language, More says:
"Why am I beginning to think like Fr. Smith?" (339). Although
More has never been to Germany, the priest has, and this dou-
bling indicates a degree of melding of the consciousnesses of the
two men. But this is only the beginning of a series of complex
relationships between the two episodes.

Tom's trip to Pantherburn began with a series of *deja vus*
that indicated his growing disjunction from time; Fr. Smith's
Confession begins with the priest telling More about another
kind of temporal disjunction. "It was not a dream but a complete return of an experience which was real in every detail—as
if I were experiencing it again" (235). What Fr. Smith experienced was a repetition, and its originating details, strikingly similar to More's experience at Pantherburn, reveals Percy's obvious
paralleling of the two episodes. The dark pines beneath his fire
tower recall to the priest ". . . the Schwarzwald with its dark firs
. . . I've told you about it before" (236). He remembers his trip to
Turbingen as a youth, "lying in bed in my cousin's house . . . listening to the sound of church bells" which give off "a high-
pitched silvery sound, almost like crystal struck against crystal."
He recalls a "sweet" smell like "old geraniums," as he lay "in a
narrow bed covered not by a blanket or a quilt but by a soft goose-
down bolster, like a light mattress. It was like an old-fashioned
Southern feather bed with the mattress upside down. There was
also the vague but certain sense that something was about to
happen" (326). And just as Lucy put her hand on Tom "like the
touch of a friend at a funeral" just before giving him the "sweet
sorrow" news of Ellen's infidelity, so also Fr. Smith places a
"talon" of a hand on Tom with "sweet urgency before telling his
confession," reminding More of "the time a priest came to get
me out of a classroom to tell me my father was dead" (238).

All of these images, plus the similar sense of foreboding
premonition, echoes Tom's experience at Pantherburn. But the
episodes are also different in crucial ways. First of all, Fr.
Smith's memory is of an *actual* personal experience, not like
Tom's fantasy of a tryst with Alice Pratt in the Schwarzwald.
Secondly, as I noted, the priest's confession is a coherent,
straight-forward examination, the purpose of which is to penetrate the meaning of his experience; this is not the disjointed
ramblings of a Tom. Moreover, the priest seeks the past in order
to guide the present, for the real purpose of his confession is to
give More insight into *his* actions in the present. "I'm afraid

this concerns you," (he tells Tom as the outset). "I didn't want to
tell you, but I'm afraid I have to. There is something you need
to know" (238). The priest's confession, then, is "good" bad
news, a help to clarify Tom's decisions. Whereas Lucy's news
about Ellen's infidelity led More to drinking, despair and adultery, Fr. Smith's will help him to a better understanding of his
role and responsibilities vis-a-vis Fedville.

The two episodes also serve to define the larger theme of
More's relation to mythological and historical conceptions of
time, and his movement from the former to the latter is I think
a clear sign of his partial spiritual revitalization. At Pantherburn
the disjointed flow of "memories"—from present to fantasized
past (Germany) to romanticized past (the Old South)—aptly signify Tom's separation from and confusion over real historical
experience. Tom's mental equating of these "events" indicates
that closed pattern of *cyclical* repetition which is inherent in a
mythological conception of time and events.[7] In the priest's
confession, however, More hears a coherent exposition of the
moral significance of past events in the priest's life as they relate
to necessary actions in the present—Tom's need "to choose—life
or death." In this sense, Fr. Smith's exegesis amounts to a
redemption of time and the past, producing insights that help
More escape from the confusing solipsism he experienced at
Pantherburn. This is a paradigm of the Christian idea of time,
and of man's creative action in history to further the redemptive
process. (It may also be a clue to the melioration of evil Percy attempts in disposing of the euthanasists and pedophiles at the
end of the novel, all of them "better off.") A closer look at the
confession itself will substantiate this.

Fr. Smith's confession is nothing less than a careful and
painful reexamination of his past life to discover his own moral
responsibility in history. His father was incurably romantic, an
"upholder" of Southern culture and lofty "ideals," a humanitarian enamored of romantic pre-war Germany. His mother was a
Catholic New Orleans socialite both "pious and hostile" who
had masses said for those who offended her. Fr. Smith grew up
disaffected from both parents, and he became a priest even
though he claims to dislike everyone except "bums, outcasts,
pariahs, family skeletons, and the dying" (243). In the process,
like More, he became an alcoholic. Yet the crucial event in his
life was the visit to Germany where, as he came to see, he underwent his own "fall" into history. He now recognizes what

was then his own love of death in his readiness to join his cousin Helmut in the SS and "sacrifice all" for country—"The flag and death."

> . . . This is my confession. If I had been German not American, I would have joined him. I would not have joined the distinguished Weimar professors. I would not have joined the ruffian Sturmabteilung. I would not have matriculated at the University of Turbingen or Heidelberg. I would not have matriculated at Tulane, as I did, and joined the DKE's. I would have gone to the Junderschule, sworn the solemn oath of Teutonic Knights of Marienberg, and joined the Schutzstaffel. Do you hear me? *I would have joined them.* (248)

Fr. Smith's insight into his own love of death comes through an understanding of the meaning of historical events, specifically the link between the Nazi experience, the Fedville projects, and the meaning of the Jewish-Christian event. In the 1930's, he could not make "head or tails" of the significance of the Jews; ideas of a "Judaic conspiracy" expressed by his cousin Helmut made no sense to him. Only after the war, after discovering Dr. Jager's role in exterminating children at Dachau, does Fr. Smith grasp "the connection" between the romantic ethos of pre-war Germany and the horror of mass exterminations on ideological grounds. "Only later was I horrified," the priest admits. "We've got it wrong about horror. It doesn't come naturally but takes some effort" (254). And so when asked by More why he became a priest, Fr. Smith suggests that his vocation is related to his understanding of his German experience and the moral responsibility that it entails *now*.

> In the end one must choose—given the chance.
> Choose what?
> Life or death. What else? (257)

Tom More's reaction to the priest's confession, however, is not explicitly clear. He seems more interested in Fr. Smith's "memory" as a psychological experience, a hallucination induced by mental or neurological disorder. At the end of the first confession, in fact, More says: "I don't understand"; and even when Smith adds his Footnote about Dr. Jager's experiments at Dachau, More says: "I'm not sure what you're trying to tell me—about your memory—about Germany" (256). Fr. Smith presses the point:

> Could I ask you a question, Tom?
> Sure.

> Do you think we're different from the Germans?
> I couldn't say. I hope so.
> Do you think present day Soviet psychiatrists are any
> different from Dr. Jager and that crowd?
> I couldn't say. But what is the point, Father? (256)

Yet even when Fr. Smith makes the point by saying one must choose between life and death, More's thoughts are elsewhere.

> What else. I'm thinking of the smell of geraniums and
> of the temporal lobe where smells are registered and, in
> some cases of epilepsy or brain tumor, replay, come back
> with all the halting force of memory. And play one
> false too. I don't recall geraniums having a smell. (257)

While More may *seem* to have possibly missed the point of Fr. Smith's confession, it is important I think to look beyond his laconic response and examine his actual deeds. Though his words here bespeak the viewpoint of a scientist, More's subsequent actions reveal profound signs of Fr. Smith's influence, though to preserve dramatic consistency Percy does not "say" this explicitly.

More does not discuss his reaction to Fr. Smith's confession and the warning that he must choose between "life and death," but Tom's actions in the novel's resolution do indeed suggest that he "chooses life." First of all, Percy puts the emphasis upon Tom's *actions* after the Pantherburn episode; no longer is he afflicted by overpowering *deja vus* of the past. His gaze is fixed upon *what needs to be done in the present time*—here and now. There is of course his thwarting of the Blue Boy plot and the saving of the children at Belle Ame. In addition, there is his reconciliation with Ellen and his choice of a humble, even failing medical practice (which includes volunteer work at St. Margaret's Hospice) instead of a high-paying job at Fedville. Equally important is More's recognition of the "thanatos" represented by Lucy Lipscomb and life at Pantherburn. After reporting her reconciliation with Buddy Dupre, Tom says:

> It is just as well. I'd have gotten into trouble with Lucy,
> lovely as she is in her bossy-nurturing, mothering-
> daughtering way, always going *tch* and fixing some-
> thing for me, brushing off dandruff with quick rough
> brushes of her hand, spitting on her thumb to smooth
> my eyebrows. The one time she came to my bed, coming
> somewhat over and onto me in an odd, agreeable, early-
> morning incubus centering movement, I registered, along
> with the pleasant centering weight of her, the inkling
> that she was the sort who likes the upper hand. . . .
> She, Lucy, gave signs of wanting to marry me, and how

> could I have not. . . . An unrelieved disaster it would
> have been, what with her uncle calling ducks night and
> day and what with Ellen coming home eventually. I'd
> have ended up for sure like our common ancestor, Lucy's
> and mine, with one wife too many in a great old house,
> sunk in English Tory melancholy, nourishing paranoid
> suspicions against his neighbors, fearful of crazy Yan-
> kee Americans coming down the river (Como and com-
> pany) and depraved French coming up the river (Buddy
> Dupre and the Cajuns)—in the end seeing no way out but
> to tie a sugar kettle on his head and jump into the river.
> (348)

John Edward Hardy, who claims that Tom fears Lucy as a dominant, intelligent and independent woman, sees his escape from her as a sign of weakness (238-239). Perhaps this is true, but even if so, it does not seem to me to disqualify More's insight that *for him*, life with Lucy at Pantherburn would be a disaster. It is also significant that Tom sees a life with Lucy in terms of a cyclical repetition of the ancestral pattern, with its romantic mythos, one that literally is a "dead-end," and instead chooses "life" in the present, moving forward into an uncertain future. The alternative Tom sees and rejects is clear: spiritual and literal suicide.

While More's connection with the thanatos world of the Pantherburn Lipscombs is diminished near the novel's end, his bond with Fr. Smith is strengthened. More importantly, this link with the priest is cast specifically in terms of the mythologi-cal-historical theme and the meaning of time in the Judeo-Chris-tian perspective. Percy suggests this in several ways. First of all, although Tom *seems* indifferent to his own nominal Catholi-cism, he nevertheless participates on occasion in the masses said by Fr. Smith, and as a personal favor serves willingly when asked. More also performs the paternal duty of taking his chil-dren to Mass on Christmas, insisting, when Ellen protests, that "after all Meg and Tom are Catholics" (355). Moreover, he im-plicitly defends the validity of the Catholic sacraments when, in answer to Ellen's claim that they must be "born again," Tom replies; "I thought I was born again when I was baptized." But perhaps the most important sign of More's direction is his final "link" with Fr. Smith in the novel—a coded message from the priest to come because tomorrow is "The Feast of the Epiphany. A Jewish girl, a visit from royalty. Gifts" (370).

Percy's emphasis upon the feast of the Epiphany con-summates the theme of disjunction from time and the mytho-

logical-historical tension because the Epiphany is a feast celebrated within a liturgical conception of time and event. That is,
the celebration is both temporal and transcendent; it is the repetition of an event which has been transformed by its assimila-
tion into a Christian concept of historical time, one that links
past (the original Epiphany) with present (its sacred reenactment
here and now). Eliade explains the matter as follows:

> Origen rightly understood that the originality of
> Christianity lies above all in the fact that the Incar-
> nation took place in a historical Time and not in cosmic
> Time. . . . In proclaiming the Incarnation, Resurrection,
> and Ascension of the Word, the Christians were sure
> that they were not putting forth a new myth.
>
> It must be at once added that, *by the very fact that
> it is a religion*, Christianity had to keep at least one
> mythical aspect—liturgical time, that is, the periodi-
> cal recovery of the *illud tempus* of the 'beginnings.' The
> religious experience of the Christian is based upon an
> *imitation* of the Christ as *exemplary pattern*, upon the
> liturgical repetition of the life, death, and resurrection
> of the Lord, and upon the *contemporaneity* of the Chris-
> tian with the *illud tempus* which begins with the Na-
> tivity at Bethlehem and end, provisionally, with the
> Ascension. . . .
>
> However, though liturgical Time is circular Time,
> Christianity, as faithful heir to Judaism, accepts the
> linear Time of History: the World was created only
> once and will have only one end; the Incarnation took
> place only once, in historical time, and there will be
> only one Judgement.[8]

Time and history are redeemed and redeemable in this Christian
vision, and More's suggested link to it at the end of the novel is
vitally important. No longer is he prey to the kind of disjunction of time he suffered at Pantherburn; now he acts in the present to create a better order of existence by ministering to the
needs of others.[9]

In a larger sense, too, the image of the Epiphany con-
summates the link Percy implies between the Germany of the
1930's and the Louisiana of time present. The Epiphany, celebrat-
ing the entrance of Christ into the world, is an event tied directly
to the meaning of history and the Jews. History begins with the
Jews. The Epiphany, then, is a counter-symbol to the mythic disjunction of time under which the Nazis perpetrated their unspeakable assaults on human dignity. Nazism is based on a
myth, as Fr. Smith claims, a false "ideal" of human perfectability

which ruthlessly opposes the real history of man's fallen state, and his capacity for redemption by Christ. Hence Nazism chose as prime target of its insane "purification" that people intimately connected with the "Jewish-Christian Event" which is celebrated in the Epiphany. In a novel that is quintessentially about signs, and the devaluation of signs in the modern world, the Epiphany stands as a sign of the indestructible hope that emerged from the Jewish-Christian event, and a sign of Tom's crucial, life-giving choice to return to the suffering reality of time and history.

Notes

[1] Percy, Walker. *The Thanatos Syndrome*. New York: Farrar, Straus and Giroux, 1987, pp. 239-257. All further references cited in the text.

[2] Hardy, John Edward. *The Fiction of Walker Percy*. Urbana: University of Illinois Press, 1987, pp. 225-233. All further references cited in the text.

[3] It may be that the technique of disjunction Percy uses in this episode is a heightened version of the general disjunction of chronology and location in the novel, noted by Hardy. In effect, the overall technique suggests that Percy wishes to emphasize a pervasive loss of time-place sense in modern society, again apropos the theme of the relationship between myth and history.

[4] Eliade, Mircea. *The Sacred and the Profane*. New York: Harcourt, Brace and World, 1957, pp. 110-112. All further references cited in the text.

[5] Lawson, Lewis A. and Victor A. Kramer. *Conversations with Walker Percy*. Jackson: University Press of Mississippi, 1985, p. 13. All further references cited in the text.

[6] Hardy has noted the association between the two scenes, and the peculiar "stuff floating around in Tom's consciousness" from earlier conversations with Fr. Smith. Hardy does not, however, develop the close parallels, though he does acknowledge that the confession is decisive in leading More to action against the Fedville plotters. See Hardy 246-249.

[7] See Eliade, pp. 88-99.

[8] Eliade, Mircea. *Myth and Reality*. New York: Harper and Row, 1963, pp. 168-169.

[9] In the last scene in the novel, More is helping Mickey LaFaye in her attempt to identify a "terrifying stranger" who enters her dreams to "tell her something." The stranger seems to be in one sense Mickey's true self. But might it not also be the "terrifying stranger" who entered history to bring it "good news" and whose "showing forth" to the world is celebrated in the Epiphany? Or might not the stranger be both?

Walker Percy's Triad:
Science, Literature and Religion

Walker Percy's novels, essays, and interviews express the views of a writer interested in developing an integral vision of what it means to live as a human being in the disordered twentieth century. As a thinker Percy found himself placed in a world in which ways of knowing—scientific versus poetic, empirical versus intuitive, etc.—had come to be seen as separate if not entirely antithetical. For Percy, this situation was due mainly to the pervasive influence of a corrupt form of science, called "scientism," in all areas of life. The task he set about in his writings was to demonstrate the epistemological coherence which he believed was attainable by the modern mind through the study of the human use of language. This attainable coherence would make possible a reunification of an authentic scientific viewpoint and the arts. Percy's whole career can be seen as an attempt to undermine the regnant ideology of scientism, on the one hand, and on the other, to heal the rift between science and the arts by demonstrating that, although they approach the truth in different ways, science and the arts are wholly compatible because they share an integral metaphysical foundation. Both science and the arts are concerned with the search for truth, and truth, Percy said, echoing the Scholastics, cannot contradict itself.

In his essay entitled "The Fateful Rift: The San Andreas Fault in the Modern Mind," Percy offered one way to heal this rift when he suggested that contemporary social scientists should emulate the artist's approach to the study of human experience. Speaking of literature in general, he said:

> . . . these 'sentences' of art, poetry, and the novel ought to be taken very seriously indeed since these are the cognitive, scientific, if you will, statements that we have about what it is to be human. The humanities, in

a word, are not the minstrels of the age whose role is to promise 'R and R' to tired technicians and consumers after work. Rather are the humanities the elder brother of the sciences, who see how the new scientist got his tail in a crack when he takes on the human subject as object and who even shows him the shape of a new science.[1]

Percy's claim for the cognitive, scientific value of literature as a norm for the fully human was rooted in his belief in man's uniqueness as a creature who symbolizes. Human beings are namers who are capable of discovering truths about reality, which exists independent of mind and can be defined with reasonable accuracy. Yet literature and science approach truth in different ways. The goal of the scientist, Percy argued, is to express a "general truth" about things and events. However, science cannot express the truth about a unique existence. "The great gap in human knowledge to which science cannot address itself by the very nature of the scientific method is . . . nothing less than this: what it is like to be an individual, to be born, live, and die in the twentieth century" (*Signposts*, 151). The individual writer, however, can address the question because "he finds himself in league with the individual, with his need to have himself confirmed in his predicament" (151). Still, Percy's insistence on the "cognitive, scientific" value of literature implies a single metaphysical foundation for the two ways of knowing and expressing truth. In effect, Percy's Jefferson Lecture was a call for a radical reintegration of science, the arts, and—I believe—religion, by a reconsideration of their epistemological root in the nature of being itself, discoverable through the study of language. Paradoxically, Percy saw this reintegration as possible for some educated citizens only after a thorough absorption of the scientific method: ". . . it is *only* through, first, the love of the scientific method and, second, its elevation and exhaustion as the ultimate method of knowing that he becomes open to other forms of knowing—sciencing in the root sense of the word—and accordingly, at least I think so, to a new kind of revival of Western humanism and the Judeo-Christian tradition . . ." (*Signposts*, 192). Percy's belief in the possibility of this revival underpins his whole epistemological journey as philosopher and writer.

To understand Percy's argument for reintegration, certain basic terms need to be clarified. Like Charles Sanders Peirce, Percy understood the term "science" and the act of "sciencing" to mean any search for knowledge about being and existence with the aim of uncovering demonstrable truth.[2] "Science" in this sense has as much to do with ontological perspective as with a specific method; specific method is governed by the first principles from which it derives. Percy reaffirmed this basic notion of science against the degenerate scientism which claimed authority in all areas of life. In his essay "Physician as Novelist" he distinguished ". . . between scientism as an all-pervading ideology and the scientific method as a valid means of investigating the mechanisms of phenomena . . ." (192), while in an earlier essay, "Culture: The Antinomy of Scientific Method," Percy noted how allegiance to scientism precludes consideration of science's deeper, ontological basis: "Once the scientific method is elevated to a supreme all-construing world view, it becomes impossible to consider a more radical science, the science of being."[3] Scientism exists as one of the major idols of the modern Western world, manifested particularly in popular interest in the occult and the magical. This interest, for Percy, represented "a loss of interest in science in favor of pseudo-science" (323). But paradoxically, he believed that "one happy outcome of this turn of events may well be a new alliance of science and religion, such as existed in medieval times against the old and new Gnosticism which periodically threatens the openness and catholicity of both science and Christianity with its appeal to the occult and mystical powers of the elite few" (323).

As for the terms "religion" or "religious," Percy shied away from using them whenever possible because he believed such terms had become devalued almost beyond usefulness. In fact, in the Jefferson Lecture he argued that the "sciences of man are incoherent" and that "the solution to the difficulty is not to be found in something extra-scientific, not in the humanities nor in religion, but within science itself" (271). Percy wished to avoid grounding his argument for a "new anthropology" in a crippling dependence on worn-out definitions of science, religion, and the arts. But characteristically, he turned to etymology in his attempt to reaffirm their authentic relationship. Just as he referred to the root meaning of the word "science" (*scio*=to know) to affirm its true sense, so also he defined "incoherence" in its root sense of a "not sticking together." Following his strategy, I would argue that the term "religious" understood in its root sense—"to bind fast and hold together"—is both appropriate and necessary to understand the kind of integral vision of art and science Percy wished to describe, in spite of his claim that the solution to the incoherence in modern social sciences is *not* to be found in religion.

More importantly, I believe his proposed reintegration of science and art would itself be incoherent without the synthesizing power of a religious perspective—and a specifically Christian perspective at that. Percy's claim that genuine science's coherence does not depend on religion is accurate in the strict sense, I think. But since he goes on to argue that coherence can be found through semiotics—the study of man as a language user—the question of the ontological roots of language, and hence the religious, is inevitably raised. That is, the question of language's ultimate source and authority to define being must be addressed if the notion of "coherence" is finally to have any validity.

Percy's triadic view of language and his indebtedness to Charles Sanders Peirce are by now so well known that restatement seems unnecessary, but a few ideas crucial to this discussion bear emphasizing. Peirce's semiotic philosophy is a modern variation of the position of realists in the critical nominalist-realist debate over language that took place within medieval Scholasticism. Realism ". . . is predicated upon the equal reality of the ideas and of actuality. There are ideas apart from the things that partake of them. . . . The ideas are not mere abstractions; they are essences, essences being only another name for intelligible and incorporeal ideas. . . Names are intended to show the nature of things."[4] Nominalism, on the other hand, is "predicated upon the superiority of actuality. Man is the measure of all things. . . . There is no principle in name. Names as truth are nonsense . . ." (447). In "The Principles of Phenomenology" Peirce vigorously attacked the nominalist position and in response offered his own concept of thirdness to defend the validity of universals, a concept derived in part from the realism of Duns Scotus. As for Percy, although he does not say so explicitly, it is obvious from his allegiance to Peirce's semiotic and from his satirical attacks in fiction against the confusions wrought by modern nominalists (especially in *Love in the Ruins* and *The Thanatos Syndrome*) that he regarded it as a major symptom of the incoherence in the modern mind. Language, Percy remarked, is the pathology of the twentieth century.

The realist position on language is rooted in an essentialism that affirms human language as the medium between mind and independent existent reality, whose intelligible form can be known—indirectly—and named. According to the Scholastics, knowledge of essences is mediated by symbols. In "The Mystery of Language," Percy noted that "The Scholastics . . . used to say that man does not have a direct knowledge of essences as do the angels but only an indirect knowledge, a knowledge mediated by symbols. John of St. Thomas observed that symbols come to contain within themselves the thing symbolized *in alio esse*, in another mode of existence" (*Message*, 156). The realist position thus affirms the non-material as both real and definitive of being. Percy insisted repeatedly that the act of naming—the mysterious joining of object, namer, and word-sign by a copula—is a real, non-material act. He also argued that Peirce's triadic theory, based on realism, offers a solution "within science itself" to the present incoherence in the social sciences because its emphasis on man as symbol-maker offers a unique, integral perspective from which to examine and gauge human behavior.

Percy does not trace out the links between Peirce's semiotic theory, the realism of medieval Scholastics, and the theological roots of language, but if he had, I believe he would have arrived at a point where the affirmation of the Divine Logos as the absolute ground for the realist position would have been inevitable. In the Jefferson Lecture he wished to remain strictly within the purview of science. But from an epistemological viewpoint the realist position—that universals name real essences which exist independent of mind—is finally insupportable without affirming the reality of an ultimate source of Being and human knowledge. The validity of universal concepts, and their knowability, rests ultimately upon their participation in the original forms of ideas in the mind of God. This, it seems to me, is the religious core, the "that which binds together," of Percy's entire argument.

Percy's linguistic realism is also at the core of his belief in the intrinsic link between Christianity, a genuine scientific method, and the practice of literature, and hence at the center of his hope for a reintegration of science, religion and the arts. In "Another Message in the Bottle" he insisted on the theological and historical connection between Christianity and novel-writing.

> It is no coincidence that in the very part of the world where novels have been written and read, the presiding ethos, the central overriding belief, is that the salient truth of life is not the teaching of a great philosopher or the enlightenment of a great sage. It was, rather, the belief that something had happened, an actual

> Event in historic time. Certainly no one disagrees that
> one great difference of Christianity is its claim—outra-
> geous claim, many would say—that God actually en-
> tered historic time, first through his covenant with the
> Jews and then through the Incarnation.
>   . . . What concerns us here is the peculiar relevance
> of this belief to novel-writing. I could also speak of its
> relevance to the other art forms—drama and poetry for
> example—*and to the genesis of science."* (365) (My
> italics).

Percy's statement suggests the intrinsic connection between his
semiotic realism, his Christology, and his view of science and
novel-writing. Under nominalism, a universal concept such as
a definable "nature of man" is meaningless. One implication of
this is that the notion of a union of human nature and the divine nature in the Person of Christ also becomes meaningless.
A second consequence is that, in the realm of science, nominalism separates natural science from any metaphysical assumptions or ultimate principles; science is "liberated" from any such
assumptions, to deal with phenomena on their own terms.
Percy's realism, on the other hand, affirms the hypostatic union
of divine and human in the Person of Christ, whose entry into
history links the divine Word with words. In "Why are you a
Catholic?" Percy argued that there are only two signs in the post-
modern world which have not been consumed by scientistic
theory. One sign is the self; the other is the presence of the Jews.

> The only other sign in the world which cannot be en-
> compassed by theory is the Jews, their unique history,
> their suffering and achievements, what they started
> (both Judaism and Christianity), and their presence in
> the here-and-now.
>   The Jews are a stumbling block to theory. They can-
> not be subsumed under any social or political theory. . . .
> The great paradox of the Western world is that even
> though it was in the Judeo-Christian West that modern
> science arose and flourished, it is Judeo-Christianity
> which the present-day scientific set of mind finds the
> most offensive among the world's religions. (312)

By the "present day scientific set of mind" Percy of course
means scientism, and he contrasts its exaggerated claims with
the aims of legitimate science. ". . . the scientific method is correct as far as it goes, but the theoretical mind-set, which assigns
significance to single things and events only insofar as they are
examples of theory or items for consumption, is in fact an infla-

tion of a method of knowing and is unwarranted" (313). Consequently, Percy sees the Judeo-Christian belief as not only compatible with the legitimate aims of science, but in fact a source and guarantor of its epistemological coherence. In his essay "Is a Theory of Man Possible?" he proposes a new anthropology based on the science of semiotic, a semiotic rooted historically and ontologically in the Incarnation.

For Percy, then, the hypostatic Event—the coming of the divine Word into history—validates man as a symbol-maker who uses language both as scientist and as artist in his quest for truth. It is *the* specific event in history that gives ultimate ontological meaning to both the scientific and artistic enterprises. Percy frequently underscored this point, especially with reference to literature.

> The fact that novels are narratives about events which happen to people in the course of time is given a unique weight in an ethos that is informed by the belief that awards an absolute importance to an Event which happened to a Person in historic time. In a very real way, one can say that the Incarnation not only brought salvation to mankind but gave birth to the novel.
> ....
> In a word, it is my conviction that the incarnational sacramental dimensions of Catholic Christianity are the greatest natural assets of a novelist. (*Signposts*, 366)

Just as he saw a danger in the predominant influence of theory in the social science, she saw a similar potential danger for literature being subsumed by theory. "It is not too much to say, I think, that though most current novelists may not be believing Christians or Jews, they are still living in a Judeo-Christian ethos. If, in fact, they are living on the fat of the faith, so to speak, one can't help wonder what will happen when the fat is consumed. Perhaps there are already signs. Witness the current loss of narrative of character and events in the post-modern novel" (366).

What is unique about the novel, Percy argued, is its "narrativity and commonplaceness," and these unique qualities are everywhere affirmed by the Judeo-Christian view. In the last analysis, then, Percy's linking of realist semiotics to the Judeo-Christian event was the religious core which bound together genuine science and the arts as two aspects of the human search for meaning within the ordinary events of the world.

Notes

1 Percy, Walker. *Signposts in a Strange Land*. Ed. by Patrick Samway. New York: Farrar, Straus and Giroux, 1991, p. 288. All further references cited in the text.

2 *Signposts*, p. 151.

3 Percy, Walker. *The Message in the Bottle*. New York: Farrar, Straus and Giroux 1975,.

4 Peirce, Charles Sanders. *Essays in the Philosophy of Sciences*. Ed. by Vincent Tornas. New York: Bobs Merrill Co., 1957, pp. 189-194.

Technology and the Other in
Walker Percy and Don Delillo

In his essay entitled "Notes for a Novel about the End of the World," Walker Percy defined the problem of the religious seeker in our modern technological society in the following way:

> The proper question is not whether God has died or been superceded by the urban-political complex. The question is not whether the Good News is no longer relevant, but whether it is possible that man is presently undergoing a tempestuous restructuring of consciousness which does not presently allow him to take account of the Good News. For what has happened is not merely the technological transformation of the world but something psychologically even more portentous. It is the absorption by the layman not of the scientific method but rather of the magical aura of science, whose credentials he accepts for all sectors of reality. Thus in the lay culture of a scientific society nothing is earlier than to fall prey to a kind of seduction which sunders one's very self from itself into an all-transcending 'objective' consciousness and a consumer self with a list of 'needs' to be satisfied. It is this monstrous bifurcation of man into angelic and bestial components against which old theologies must be weighed before new theologies are erected. Such a man could not take account of God, the devil, and the angels if they were standing before him, because he has already peopled the universe with his own hierarchies.[1]

In Percy's novels *Love in the Ruins* and *The Thanatos Syndrome*, Father Rinaldo Smith states the problem more succinctly when he says: "The airwaves are jammed." Percy's technological image for our literal distraction from ourselves and the possibility of hearing the Good News echoes Don Delillo's vision of the numbing effects of modern culture's pervasive "static" in his brilliant novel, *White Noise*.

Percy's belief that our allegiance to the magical aura of science and technology produces a radical separation of the human self from its true being is of course a view of alienation shared by many modern theologians, philosophers, and novelists. In this radical separation from true being, the self casts about for authentic existence, yet falls prey to the mock identities created by role-playing, by assuming an "objective" self, by consumerism, or by sensuality. All such paths of alienation lead the self to despair as defined by Kierkegaard, for as Percy often insisted, quoting the Danish philosopher, "the only way for self to truly become itself is by becoming itself transparently under God."[2]

Several questions emerge from Percy's observations. First, is our absorption of the magical aura of science and technology the root cause of modern alienation from true being, as Percy suggests? Secondly, if this absorption has produced a "tempestuous restructuring of consciousness" which prevents us from hearing the Good News, can the self recover from this radical estrangement from being? Stated differently: can the self be healed of its own experience of otherness? If so, how? Kierkegaard's belief that the self could only become itself "transparently under God" affirms at least the possibility of such a healing. But Percy's argument about the pervasive effects of scientism suggests an almost unbridgeable gap between the modern consciousness and the ability to hear the Good News. Some clues to answers to these questions may be found, I believe, by a comparison of Delillo's treatment of alienation and otherness in *White Noise*, his 1984 National Book Award-winning novel, with Percy's treatment of the same condition in *Love in the Ruins* and *The Thanatos Syndrome*.

In *White Noise*, Delillo's protagonist Jack Gladney lives in a consumerist world where virtually all experience has been reduced to simulacra of reality. A professor of Hitler Studies at a midwestern college, Gladney has packaged the history of the Third Reich into a post-modern, "value-free" commodity for students whose pursuit of higher education amounts to a kind of casual voyeurism. Gladney himself has constructed his public identity around the cult of Hitler. He wears dark sunglasses and academic robes on campus, and he admits: "I am the false character that follows the name around."[3] If history has become a museum of collectibles, nature in Gladney's world has become a product for consumption. A barn near Gladney's home cannot be seen truly anymore because it has become "the most photographed barn in America." In addition to Cable News and Cable Weather, television now offers "Cable Nature."

In similar fashion, events now have to be "authenticated" by the media. A near plane crash is not real unless the media covers it. Jack's colleague Murray Siskind plans to offer a course in "the cinema of car crashes." Sexual relations are also mediated and artificialized. Jack and his wife Babette read pornography and erotic scenes from historical novels during their lovemaking, projecting themselves into pre-fabricated roles. Technology, with its unstated belief that all defects of existence are correctible, saturates the world of *White Noise*—from television to Muzak to films and transistor radios and tape players, to the higher world of medical and pharmacological "expertise." Thus when Jack's wife becomes anxious about death, she at once searches for a miracle drug called Dylar to eliminate her anxiety.

Yet even death has become de-personalized and objectified in this technology-governed world. When Gladney is contaminated by chemical fallout from an "airborne toxic event" and asks if he is going to die, a technician tells him "not as such," although he admits: "we have a situation." When the same technician tells him "you are the sum of your data," Gladney reflects upon this form of alienation:

> Death has entered. It is inside you. You are said to be dying and yet you are separate from the dying, can ponder it at your leisure, literally see on the X-ray photographer computer screen the horrible alien logic of it all. It is when death is rendered graphically, is televised so to speak, that you sense an eerie separation between your condition and yourself. A network of symbols has been introduced, an entire awesome technology wrested from the gods. It makes you feel like a stranger in your own dying. (142)

Yet faced with the fact that he is contaminated with toxins, Gladney cannot escape awareness of his own mortality. However, neither can he fully embrace it, given the way technology has "objectified" his condition into "data." Thus the consciousness of his anomalous medical condition itself further separates him from his own reality. Awareness of his mortality is disorienting precisely because, under technology's aegis, Gladney cannot grasp its true meaning. His situation is further exacerbated by the fact that one of the effects of the "airborne toxic event" is an increase in *deja-vu* experiences among fallout victims. But these *deja-vu* experiences are aberrations of mind that lead nowhere, illusory recollections of free-floating mental "data" that only intensify alienation.

What possible avenues of spiritual recovery seem open in Delillo's novel to one who has become "a stranger in his own dying"? Gladney tries various ways to deal with his self-estrangement. He retreats to the womb-like comfort of sexual intimacy with Babette, but the retreat is soon invaded by Babette's own anxiety over death. He tries to identify more with his unself-conscious son Wilder, but he cannot really return to Wilder's world of childhood innocence. He searches for the wonder drug Dylar—the death placebo—only to discover it doesn't exist.

Then in desperation he follows his colleague Siskind's advice that the way to achieve power over death is by committing acts of violence. Gladney aims to murder the amorphous Mr. Gray (*aka* Willie Mink), the dispenser of Dylar who seduced Babette, but the plan is botched and both Gladney and his intended victim end up in a hospital staffed by German nuns. Here, Gladney waxes nostalgically over a picture of John Kennedy and the Pope in heaven, and asks the nun: "Is it still the old heaven, like that, in the sky?" "Do you think we are stupid?" replies the nun. Shocked, Gladney asks why she is a nun if she doesn't believe, and she answers:

> It is for others. . . . The others who spend their lives believing that *we* still believe. . . . If we did not pretend to believe these things, the world would collapse.
>
> Our pretense is a dedication. Someone must appear to believe. Our lives are no less serious than if we profess real faith, real belief. As belief shrinks from the world, people find it more necessary than ever that *someone* believe. Wild-eyed men in caves. Nuns in black. Monks who do no speak. We are left to believe. Fools, children. Those who have abandoned belief must still believe in us. They are sure that they are right not to believe but they know belief must not fade completely. Hell is when no one believes. (318-319)

When Gladney then asks the nun about death and the afterlife ("And nothing survives? Death is the end?"), her answer is further confounding:

> 'Do you want to know what I believe or what I pretend to believe?'
> 'I don't want to hear this. This is terrible.'
> "But true.'—she answers.

The last scene in *White Noise* shows Gladney watching a sunset from an overpass outside town, a kind of eerie coda to the novel's post-modern world. Gladney seems to have accepted his own estranged humanity and his dying. But in terms of finding any hope for meaning, viewing a sunset seems a small consolation in a world inundated with the white noise of technology to the point where all seem alienated from their own living. Any path to spiritual healing seems a lost trace in the universe.

Delillo's novel would seem to confirm Percy's argument that the "tempestuous restructuring of consciousness" brought about by science and technology alienates us from selfhood and the Good News. To be a "stranger in (one's) own dying" may be the bitterest experience of alienation and otherness.

Percy's own novels, especially *Love in the Ruins* and *The Thanatos Syndrome*, dramatize the spiritually lethal effects of scientism as thoroughly as does Delillo's *White Noise*. In both novels the Federal complex—Fedville—which attempts to "objectivity" and control all human responses—from childhood to love to death—through technological manipulation and drugs serves as a stark microcosm of our modern technocentric society. Even more than Jack Gladney, Percy's Dr. Tom More in *Love in the Ruins* seems lost in an infatuation with technology's power to manipulate reality, seen especially in his plan to invent a machine to diagnose and eventually cure the fall of man. And as in the case of Gladney, it takes a personal encounter with his own mortality—More's attempted suicide—to help him begin to understand his spiritual predicament. However, Percy concentrates more on the inward journey of his heroes when faced with the collapse of the false self than does Delillo in *White Noise*. In tracing this inward journey—a journey conducted through memory—Percy suggests a path to recovery of the self from alienation, and escape from the "tempestuous restructuring of consciousness" wrought by scientism. The paradigm for this healing journey is not some secularly humanistic program of psychic reintegration. Rather it is the age-old path taken by St. Augustine in his search for God. In a religious context, any serious discussion of Otherness must I think have as its starting point our relationship with the One who is both totally within and absolutely Other—God—and the *locus classicus* for that discussion is Book Ten of St. Augustine's *Confessions*.

In *White Noise* one devastating psychological effect of the "airborne toxic event" is a dramatic increase in *deja-vu* experiences—that is, the illusion of having previously experienced an event. The effect, as I have noted, is an intensification of the alienation of the victims from the reality of their own minds. Delillo's connection of *deja-vu* experiences with a chemical disaster and pharmacological manipulation suggests a troubling fact about the *zeitgeist* of technology—its artificializing, abstracting, and disorienting of personal human memory in the name of immanence and immediacy. Memory becomes less a living and life-giving force—the actual spiritual battleground of who we are—and more like a sanitized record of information to be stored on a disk. As the technician tells Jack Gladney, "you are the sum of your data."

Not so in the case of Dr. Tom More. In *Love in the Ruins*, after his attempted suicide, More is haunted by the memory of his dead daughter Samantha, especially the memory of their attending Mass and receiving communion together while on trips. His memory, as he acknowledges, is "the thread in the labyrinth" (241) that keeps returning him to Samantha and to himself until, in the climax of the novel, he confronts his guilt for having used Samantha's death as an excuse to despair. At the same time, he recalls her warning to him not to commit the sin against grace by refusing the grace to believe in and love God. Thus, when his gnostic scientific project to heal the fall of man ends in ruins, Dr. More is able to begin his spiritual recovery, as St. Augustine was ready to begin his when his belief in gnosticism and Manicheanism began to crumble. In both cases, personal memory is the central power in the self's search for God, and for coming to recognize a true self "transparently under God." Dr. More's incipient journey toward spiritual recovery—to reconciliation to himself and to God—is underscored in the epilogue of the novel when he goes to confession to Fr. Smith, since confession itself is the sacrament of memory.

What is at issue here in Dr. More's confrontation with his own sins is a recognition of the alienating "other" within himself—that is, the forces of evil—that have caused his spiritual estrangement. But like St. Augustine, Dr. More can begin to recover true being by searching in memory for that ultimate, elusive, yet true Other, the One who is both within and beyond him—God Himself. In Percy's last novel, *The Thanatos Syndrome*, that search is more explicitly developed in the stunning confession of Fr. Rinaldo Smith about his relationship to the Germany that produced the Holocaust.

In his confession, Fr. Smith describes a visit he and his father took to Germany in the 1930's to visit distant cousins. One relative, Dr. Hans Jager, was an eminent professor of psychiatry at Tubingen. The young Smith was befriended by Dr. Jager's eighteen-year-old son Helmut, a member of the Hitler Jugend just beginning officer training school with the SS. Smith becomes enamored of all the romantic trappings of power associated with Helmut and the SS—the SS uniform with the German eagle and the death's head insignia, the marching and singing, the *Mutprobe* (test of courage), the worship of the flag, and the bayonette etched with the phrase "Blood and Iron" that Helmut gives Smith as a present. Recalling the experience for Tom More now, Fr. Smith reaches the chilling point of his confession: that given the opportunity, he would have joined his cousin Helmut in the SS and pledged his loyalty to the Third Reich to the death. Then, in a footnote to the confession, Fr. Smith describes how later as a soldier with Patton's Third Army he helped liberate Elgfing-Haar, an infamous hospital outside Munich where, as part of psychiatric and medical experiments, children were exterminated by German doctors and nurses. Smith discovers that his relative Dr. Jager was one of the doctors involved. Still, he is not immediately horrified. "Only later was I horrified," he says. "We've got it wrong about horror. It doesn't come naturally but it takes some effort" (254).

The medical experiments done to eliminate so-called "defective" human beings, motivated in part by the influential book called *The Release for the Destruction of Life Devoid of Meaning*, represents of course the ultimate perversion of technology in the service of eliminating those branded as Other—those with "defects" such as mongolism, severe epilepsy, mental retardation, schizophrenia, senility, alcoholism, and eventually, political dissidents, gypsies, Catholic opposition, and most of all—Jews. That we are in danger of forgetting the horrific premises upon which these exterminations were initiated—and technology's key role in carrying out those premises—is underscored by Percy through Fr. Smith's connection of the activities of these German doctors in the 1930's with those of the American physicians experimenting on human subjects at Fedville in the contemporary world of the novel. As Fr. Smith tells Tom, they will end up by killing Jews. And the same romantic infatuation with power, the same relinquishing of personal responsibility for identification with a cult, can be seen both in the young Smith's attraction to the Nazi movement and in the cultic attraction of young students to Hitler Studies in Delillo's *White Noise*.

Fr. Smith's confession, his searching in memory, reveals other personal failings—his general dislike of humanity, his spite, his alcoholism. So strong is his pessimism over the state of contemporary America, which he now believes is in the grip of Satan, that he retreats to a fire tower like St. Simeon the Stylite awaiting the divine intervention to come. Almost the only company he can stand—besides Tom More and his friend Milton—is the company of the dying, because they do not lie to each other. And yet at the end of the novel, we find Fr. Smith returning to the world to minister to the dying at St. Margaret's Hospice, and preparing to say Mass on the Feast of the Epiphany with Dr. Tom More as server. As Tom's wife Ellen unwittingly says, "I think it's a valuable connection for you" (370).

Fr. Smith's confession in *The Thanatos Syndrome* is a journey in memory similar to that undertaken by St. Augustine in *The Confessions*, and as such it is a clue to the self's capacity to discover its true being transparently under God. Painful and difficult, this journey nevertheless has the power—the power of grace—to heal the rift in the self, the dissociation of the self from true being, and from God—which though not *caused* by technology (original sin is the cause) is certainly exacerbated by its destructive power. In his searching through memory Fr. Smith discovers the truth about the regnant evils of the 20th century, and the truth about his own brokenness. In Book Ten of *The Confessions* Augustine says to God: ". . . you have always been present in my memory. . . . You are Truth, and you are everywhere present where all seek counsel of you."[4] Fr. Smith's confrontation with Truth in his memory, and with his own failures teaches him compassion for the brokenness of others, especially those most rejected, most in need of charity. In them he sees the mysterious image of a God who is both immanent and totally Other, and whose reality is revealed in the sacrament he is about to celebrate in the Mass of the Epiphany.

Notes

[1] Percy, Walker. *The Message in the Bottle*. New York: Farrar, Straus and Giroux, 1975, p. 113.

2 Lawson, Lewis A. and Victor A. Kramer, eds. *Conversations with Walker Percy.* Jackson, Mississippi: University Press of Mississippi, 1985, p. 49.

3 Delillo, Don. *White Noise.* New York: Penguin Books, 1984, p. 13. All further references cited in the text.

4 St. Augustine. *The Confessions of St. Augustine.* Trans. by R. S. Pine-Coffin. New York: Penguin Classics, 1961, pp. 230-231.

Charles Sanders Peirce
and Walker Percy's Communities

During the last years of his life, Walker Percy carried on an extensive correspondence with Kenneth Laine Ketner, a philosophy professor at Texas Tech University, concerning the writings of Charles Sanders Peirce. Pursuing the study of Peirce's semiotic which had occupied him for several decades, Percy asked Ketner to help him clarify certain elements of Peirce's thought, especially his triadic theory of language. The correspondence between Percy and Ketner developed into an epistolary friendship, based on their shared interest in Peirce and their mutual respect for each other's work. The correspondence, edited by Patrick Samway S. J. and published by the University of Mississippi Press, bears the title *A Thief of Peirce: The Letters of Kenneth Laine Ketner and Walker Percy*. The title of the volume refers to an important and revealing remark Percy made in a letter dated February 27, 1989, in response to Ketner's announcement that he wanted to dedicate a new volume on Peirce he was editing, *Reasoning and the Logic of Things*, to Percy. Percy responded:

> As you well know, I am not a student of Peirce. I am a thief of Peirce. I take from him what I want and let the rest go, most of it. I am only interested in CSP insofar as I understand his attack on nominalism and his rehabilitation of Scholastic realism. . . .
> But this is not the worst of it. What would set CSP spinning in his grave is the use I intend to put him to. As you probably already know, and if you don't let us keep the secret between us, I intend to use CSP as one of the pillars of a Christian apologetic. . . .
> So if you want to dedicate this book to me, please do so with the understanding that I admire at the most 1 percent of it (2 pages) and with the understanding too that it would spin CSP in his grave. Naturally I love the idea of using CSP as the foundation of a Catholic

apologetic, which I have tentatively entitled (after Aquinas) *Contra Gentiles*.[1]

Percy died a little more than a year later without fulfilling his dream to write a Peircean-based Catholic apologetic. Nevertheless, the basic argument for such a work is everywhere implicit in the Jefferson Lecture he gave at the National Endowment for the Humanities on May 3, 1989, less than three months after his letter to Ketner, entitled "The Fateful Rift: The San Andreas Fault in the Modern Mind." More importantly, it seems clear that Percy's stated intention to use Peirce's semiotic to support a Catholic apologetic not only pointed to a future project, but also revealed much of what Percy had been doing all along in his novels and essays. Percy's statement was in this respect as much a confirmation of things done as it was a prospectus for future writings. To suggest how this is so, I want to focus on the central foundation stone of Peirce's triadic semiotic—his commitment to philosophical realism—a commitment Percy shared and which became a pillar for the concept of community he developed in his novels and non-fiction writings.

Peirce's commitment to philosophical realism, or what Percy called is "reconstruction of Scholastic realism," is well-known. Setting himself in opposition to the school of nominalism, Peirce affirmed that there is a reality which exists independent of the mind which thinks it, independent of any particular cognitive act. Moreover, Peirce affirmed that generals truly exist, and that they can be known and named. For Peirce the real is both general and particular, independent of the individual mind yet capable of being known by any particular intelligence. In contrast, nominalism identifies the real with the particular and holds that generals are merely arbitrary names. The crucial point of difference between Peirce's realism and the nominalist viewpoint is that for Peirce knowledge of the real is both public and sharable, which is to say that it is rooted in the notion of community. Peirce summed up this position as follows:

> The real . . . is that which, sooner or later, information and reasoning would finally result in, and which is therefore independent of the vagaries of me and you. Thus, the very origin of the conception of reality shows that this conception involves the notion of *community*, without definite limits, and capable of a definite increase of knowledge.[2]

Joel Weinsheimer stresses the importance of this view when he says: "The idea that the real creates and depends on communities, that it is what is common to many men, and thereby makes of many one—this idea is central to Peirce's realism" (*Weinsheimer*, 249).

Since for Peirce the real is independent of the individual mind and knowable and sharable, a community of thought can attain a knowledge of true being. For Peirce, the real and the true are finally synonomous conceptions (CP 5.257). Yet how can the real be known? Peirce's full answer to this question is extraordinarily complex, involving his entire semiotic, but its essence can be summed up as follows: There is no direct knowledge of the thing in itself. All knowledge of external reality and of the self is indirect, which is to say mediated through signs. Reality is discovered (and discoverable) only through representation. Consequently semiotic—the science of signs—is at the heart of Peirce's epistemology and his concept of community. The sign is that which mediates between the object of knowledge and the knower. Since there is no direct knowledge but only through signs, Peirce's triadic principle of knowing stands at the center of the fundamental act of communication upon which community rests.

Percy expressed a similar view about the semiotic community in *Lost in the Cosmos*. Following thinkers like von Uexkull, Heidegger, and Eccles, he made a distinction between the notion of an "environment" (*Umvelt*) and a "world" (*Welt*) and affirmed that the sign-using creature inhabits a world that is based upon the realist view of generals and particulars as the foundation of community. Speaking of the sign-user in his world, Percy said:

> Yet another odd thing is that the word *apple* which you utter is part of my world but it is not a singular thing like an individual apple. It is the fact understandable only insofar as it conforms to a rule for uttering *apples*. But the oddest thing of all is your status in my world. You—Betty, Dick—are like other items in my world—cats, dogs, and apples. But you have a unique property. You are also co-namer, co-discoverer, co-sustainer of my world—whether you are Kafka whom I read or Betty who reads this. Without you—Franz, Betty—I would have no world.[3]

Percy amplified his understanding of the relation between the general and the particular, and affirmed his belief in the social significance of the realist ontology. He said:

> I will not try to decide here whether the word *apple* conjures up in your mind, its *signifie*, a percept of a concept, because it is somewhere in between. A percept refers to an individual apple. A concept is an abstraction from all apples, a definition of *apple*. But the *signifie* of *apple* is both and neither. What comes to mind when I hear *apple*, what in fact the word articulates within itself, is neither an individual apple nor a definition of *apple* but a quality of appleness, such as John Cheever intended in his title, *The World of Apples*. Perhaps it should be called a 'concrete concept' or an 'abstract percept,' or what Gerard Manley Hopkins called *inscape*.
>
> Let us take note of a notorious philosophical farrago without attempting to resolve it: Why is it that when we look at an apple, we believe that we are looking at an apple out there and not a sensory impression, a picture, in our brain? This puzzle can hardly be addressed here, since it is nothing less than the main source of the troubles which have dogged solipsist philosophers from Descartes and Locke to the present day. My own conviction is that semiotics provides an escape from the solipsist prison by its stress on the social origins of language—you have to point to an apple and name it for me before I know there is such a thing— and the existence of a world of apples outside ourselves. (*Cosmos*, 102)

One other element of Peirce's realism is especially important for understanding Percy's communities. While he affirmed that generals are real and can be known, Peirce said that what characterizes generals is indefiniteness and indeterminacy. That is, while there is a community of interpreters or sign-users whose aim is the search for the real, this community exists in a state of openness to the future. In this sense it is unlimited. Consequently the idea of *possibility* is integral to Peirce's notion of a community of interpretation. Speaking of Peirce's semiotic as a pragmatic method, Weinsheimer says:

> . . . The real consists in the habits, the beliefs, the *possible* acts of mind and body it produces. It is the idea of possibility that must be emphasized. The real consists not in what you or I or anyone or everyone thinks it is. . . . Rather the real is what all who inquire *would*

> think and *would* continue to think, if inquiry *were*
> carried far enough. (253)

Percy defined the open-ended community of the sign-used more concretely when he said:

> One's world is thus segmented by an almost unlimited
> number of signs, signifying not only here-and-now
> things and qualities and actions but also real and imag-
> inary objects in the past and future. If I wish to cata-
> logue my world, I could begin with a free association
> which could go on for months: *desk, pencil, writing,*
> *itch, Saussure, Belgian, minority, war, the end of the*
> *world, Superman, Birmingham, flying, slithy toves,*
> *General Grant, the 1984 Olympics, Lilliput, Mozart,*
> *Don Giovanni, The Grateful Dead, backing and filling,*
> *say it isn't so, dreaming. . . .*
> The nearest thing to a recorded world of signs is the
> world of H. C. Earwicker in Joyce's *Finnegans Wake.*
> (102-103)

Percy's commitment to Peircean realism and its concept of community became one of the pillars in his analysis of what he saw as the pervasive spiritual problem of the twentieth century—the alienation of the individual person. Percy saw the individual as alienated *both* from other individuals *and* from being. Furthermore, he saw the way to the recovery of being as possible only through community with another; hence only through a radical relationship. In noting the general modern condition of alienation, Percy saw both the extreme danger and the possibility of hope this situation presented. Noting with approval the theologian Romano Guardini's characterization of the post-Christian Western world, Percy said:

> (It's a world) where people are alone, but . . . it's a
> world where there is less deception; people are alone
> and, yet, they are capable of forming true relation-
> ships. One lonely person finds another lonely person.
> From this very loneliness, this existential alienation,
> there is possible a true communion, which in a way is
> even better than it used to be. . . . Even in this terrible
> twentieth century, with these terrible wars, millions of
> people being killed, till, the people I write about find a
> certain life, and it nearly always involves someone
> else. What do the French call it? *Solitude a deux.* And
> between the two they create a new world.[4]

Percy's affirmation of the possibility of a "community of two individuals," a semiotic community, can be seen in the fact that all his novels generally dramatize a movement from alienation and solipsism toward community and the public self, however tentatively. Binx Bolling's marriage to Kate Cutrer and his embarking on a medical career signifies this movement. Will Barrett's continuing link to Dr. Sutter and the Vaught family in *The Last Gentleman*, and his later love with Alison Huger and their commitment to help build the retirement community in *The Second Coming* is another example. Lance Lamar's ongoing relationship with Fr. John and Anna in *Lancelot*; Tom More's marriage to Ellen Oglethorpe in *Love in the Ruins* and his relationship with Fr. Rinaldo Smith and St. Margaret's Hospice in *The Thanatos Syndrome*; and the remnant community at Lost Cove, Tennessee in *Lost in the Cosmos*—all these can be seen as grounded in realism and the Peircean idea of an "unlimited community." In fact, the open-endedness and possibility that Peirce characterized in such a community is echoed in the very form of Percy's endings. Percy captures the inconclusiveness of life, as well as the indeterminancy of signs. The lack of closure in his endings literally embodies the realist assumptions about the nature of genuine community and of humans together in a world of open-ended signs in which we discover the future together through our mediated sign relationships.

But the difficulty, as Percy acknowledged in *Lost in the Cosmos*, is that communities are also unstable and transitory, because signs themselves are subject to devaluation and decay (although their power to name being authentically can be recovered). The problem is particularly acute in our post-religious age, Percy believed, because the traditional religious ways for the self to locate its place in the order of being in the world have been exhausted. "In a post religious, technological society, these traditional resources of the self are no longer available, leaving in general only two options: self conceived as immanent, consumer of techniques, goods, and services of society; or as transcendent, a member of the transcending community of science and art" (113). The individual may be able to temporarily escape his predicament by joining the transcending community of the scientist or the artist, but he eventually must face the problem of reentry into the ordinary world.

Yet in spite of this predicament in a post-religious age, Percy also stressed the hope—and the real possibility—of a recovery of being through community with another with both seen as creatures together under God.

> The self becomes itself by recognizing God as a spirit,
> creator of the Cosmos and therefore of one's self as a
> creature, a wounded creature but a creature nonetheless,
> who shares with a community of like creatures the be-
> lief that God, who transcends the entire Cosmos and
> has actually entered human history—or will enter it—
> in order to redeem man from the catastrophe which has
> overtaken his self. (112)

Percy's fictions are also littered with the wreckage of broken and false communities—from the Old South *noblesse oblige*
world of Binx's Aunt Emily and the elder Lamars and Barretts to
the pseudo-communities of the Vaughts New South, to Paradise
Estates and Fedville (a misguided scientific community), to
Lance's dream of a New Order in Virginia, and to the dream of a
"purified" Feliciana parish in *The Thanatos Syndrome*. Percy
saw the problem of community as pandemic in American society, yet the philosophical basis of his critique has not often been
noted, nor its logical relationship to Peircean realism. In a 1989
interview with Scott Walter, Percy observed that the post-modern, post-Christian era lacked a coherent theory of man. Percy
said that the prevailing theory offered by the media "is a kind of
pop scientific idea which . . . is fundamentally Cartesian and incoherent" (*More Conversations*, 232). Percy then linked his observation specifically to American culture.

> Tocqueville—an amazing fellow—said it 150 years ago:
> All the Americans I know are Cartesian without hav-
> ing read a word of Descartes. He meant that an edu-
> cated American believes that everything can be ex-
> plained "scientifically," can be reduced to the cause
> and effect of electrons, neutrons, and so forth. But at the
> same time, each person exempts his own mind from this,
> as scientists do. I see this endemic Cartesianism, and
> my criticism is that it leaves us without a coherent
> theory of man. Consequently, modern man is deranged.
> (*More Conversations*, 233)

The Cartesian viewpoint is completely antithetical to the
realism espoused by Peirce and Percy. Descartes's starting point
for knowledge was to doubt everything except the existence of
the thinking self: *Cogito, ergo sum*. But in doing so he presumed that the knowledge of his own thought was certain, true
knowledge. Hence his self-knowledge is deemed indubitable.
Peirce insisted that Descartes thus overlooked the possibility of
self-deception, especially when he equated clarity with certitude.
As Peirce said, "The distinction between an idea *seeming* clear

and really being so, never occurred to him" (CP 5.391). More-over, as Weinsheimer points out, "Descartes located certainty in the individual; thus he equated what he himself did not doubt with the indubitable" (247). Peirce, on the other hand, located certainty in the community of interpreters, not in the individual. Truth can be found in generals which are real, external to the individual, and which can be shared by all through the language of signs.

Percy's commitment of such a view can be seen in the central role that language, the reality of truth-telling, and the shared bond of understanding through signs occupies in his genuine communities—for example, in Val Vaught's community among the Tyree children, in the relationship between Lonnie Smith and Binx Bolling and Will Barrett and Alison Huger, and between Tom More and Fr. Smith and Fr. Smith and the dying patients of St. Margaret's Hospice. The Cartesian position, on the other hand, dooms the self to alienation because the knower presumes to stand outside of the relation and so misunderstands his real semiotic relation to the external world. This Cartesian spirit was particularly manifested, Percy recognized, in the stoic code governing the pre-modern South. As Percy noted, "It's most characteristic mood was a poetic pessimism which took a grim satisfaction in the dissolution of its values—because social decay confirmed one in his original choice of the wintery kingdom of the self."[5]

Peircean realism also provided the basis for Percy's attempt to bridge the modern gap between art and science as well as to suggest a way out of what he saw as the "incoherence" of contemporary social sciences. Both attempts presuppose Peirce's notion of an "unlimited community" of interpreters that includes both scientists and artists and is dedicated to the search for truth. As a realist Peirce saw a consonance between the activity of the scientist and the artist. He said:

> The work of the poet or novelist is not so utterly different from that of the scientific man. The artist introduces a fiction; but it is not an arbitrary one; it exhibits affinities to which the mind accords a certain approval in pronouncing them beautiful, which if it is not exactly the same as saying that the synthesis is true, is something of the same general kind. (CP 1.383; 5.535)

As Weinsheimer observes,

> . . . Peirce called into question the antithesis of the true and the beautiful, as well as that of truth and fiction.

> By definition, no fiction represents the actual, but that
> doe not preclude fiction from being true, for the true rep-
> resents the real, and the real is a category more com-
> prehensive than the actual since it includes real possi-
> bilities and real generals. Such possibilities and gener-
> alities are precisely the object of science as well as art
> insofar as science is not the intuition of the thing in it-
> self but rather the search for general laws by means of
> hypotheses, the (potentially true) fictions of science.
> (256. Also CP 5.543)

Percy likewise explored the relationship between literature and science—and their roles in the larger community of
knowledge—in several essays. In "The State of the Novel—Dying Art or New Science," Percy affirmed that art is cognitive, "as
cognitive and affirmative in its own way as science" (*Signposts*,
150). Art and science both share the power to know and express
truths about reality. However, Percy maintained that the truths
they express are different because the object of science is general
truth, whereas the object of the novelist is the truth of individual existence. As he phrased it in his well-known statement:
"The great gap in human knowledge to which science cannot
address itself is, to paraphrase Kierkegaard, nothing less than
this: What it is like to be an individual, to be born, live, and die
in the twentieth century" (*Signposts*, 151). However, while expressing the truth of individual existence, the novelist must also
capture the general condition *in* the particular, else it would be
impossible to communicate—to create a community—with the
reader. And this is what the best novels do, Percy acknowledged.
Consequently he maintained that art possesses the special power
to reverse the condition of alienation and solipsism, a condition
exacerbated by a misplaced belief in scientism as the sole definer
of reality. In the twentieth century scientism threatens to sub-
sume the individual self, but the writer stands on the side of the
individual, expressing the truth of his predicament. Percy says:

> It is the artist who at his best reverses the alienating
> process by the very act of seeing it clearly for what it is
> and naming it, and who in this same act establishes a
> kind of community. It is a paradoxical community
> whose members are both alone and yet not alone, who
> strive to become themselves and discover that there are
> others who, however tentatively, have undertaken the
> same quest. (*Signposts*, 151)

The quest Percy refers to—a quest undertaken by a paradoxical
community of individuals—is the search for personal

sovereignty. Percy's emphasis on the individual here, it seems to me, is the point at which his commitment to Peircean realism intersects with his desire to write a Catholic apologetic, precisely because of Christianity's insistence upon the absolute integrity of the individual. Stated differently, it seems to me that Percy assimilated Peirce's notion of the "unlimited community" of interpreters and signs to the Christian idea of a community (the sovereign questor's "world") that is simultaneously bound by time and space and yet open to real extensions (of meaning) that are invisible, mystical, and eschatalogical. For Percy, such a community really exist and could be embodied through signs in his novels, as when Binx talks to Lonnie Smith in *The Moviegoer*, or when at the end of the novel he assures the Smith children that Lonnie will be resurrected with a whole body at the Last Judgement. Correspondingly, Charles Peirce's inclusion of the realm of *possibility* into his definition of the real opens the way toward knowledge of such a community. Or to use Percy's image from his essay "The Message in the Bottle," realism makes it possible for us to hear the Good News because that News has already come into the world of signs and presently exists.

Percy's hope for a reconciliation of the humanities and the social sciences into a single "unlimited community" of sign-users dedicated to the pursuit of truth was expressed near the end of the Jefferson Lecture. Using Peircean realism, with its open-ended view of community, Percy prophesied a time when the artist and the scientist would be reunited in a common quest to interpret the signs of our mysterious existence as creatures in the universe. And this, he hoped, would in turn initiate a recovery of the religious. Peircean realism would create a "new anthropology" by which the triadic creature "might even explore its openness to such traditional Judeo-Christian notions as man falling prey to the worldliness of the world, and man as pilgrim seeking his salvation" (*Signposts*, 290-291). Percy's "theft" of the triadic principle from Peirce led him back to the perennial religious questions of the creature's fundamental bondedness in community to other creatures and to God. And that open-ended quest is exactly what Charles Sanders Peirce had in mind.

Notes

[1] Samway, Patrick, ed. *A Thief of Peirce: The Letters of Kenneth Laine Ketner and Walker Percy.* Jackson: University Press of Mississippi, 1955, pp. 130-131.

[2] Quoted in Joel Weinsheimer, "*The Realism of C. S. Peirce, or How Homer and Nature Can Be the Same.*" *American Journal of Semiotics*, Vol. 2, Nos. 1-2 (1983), p. 249. All further references cited in the text.

[3] Percy, Walker. *Lost in the Cosmos.* New York: Farrar, Straus and Giroux, 1983, p. 101. All further references cited in the text.

[4] Lawson, Lewis A. and Victor A. Kramer. *More Conversations with Walker Percy.* Jackson: University Press of Mississippi, 1993, p. 74.

[5] *Signposts in a Strange Land.* Edited with an introduction by Patrick Samway. New York: Farrar, Straus and Giroux, 1991, p. 85.

Index